Twayne's Theatrical Arts Series

Warren French
EDITOR

Abel Gance

Abel Gance

Abel Gance

STEVEN PHILIP KRAMER

University of New Mexico

and

JAMES MICHAEL WELSH

Salisbury State College

BOSTON

Twayne Publishers

1978

Abel Gance
is first published in 1978 by Twayne Publishers,
A Division of G. K. Hall & Co.

Copyright © 1978 by G. K. Hall & Co.

Printed on permanent/durable acid-free paper and bound
in the United States of America

First Printing, May 1978

747C9

Library of Congress Cataloging in Publication Data

Kramer, Steven Philip.
Abel Gance.

(Twayne's theatrical arts series)
Bibliography: p. 174–83.
Filmography: p. 184–95.
Includes index.
1. Gance, Abel. I. Welsh, James M., joint author.
PN1998.A3G32   791.43'0233'0924   77-25013
ISBN 0-8057-9254-6

Contents

About the Authors

Steven Philip Kramer was born in the Bronx, New York, and was educated at the Bronx High School of Science, Brandeis University, and Princeton University. At Brandeis he was editor-in-chief of the student newspaper, the *Justice*. Dr. Kramer's dissertation, researched in France, examined French politics of the Liberation (1944–46). He has taught at several universities in Maryland and currently is assistant professor of history at the University of New Mexico in Albuquerque, specializing in twentieth-century European history, French history, and intellectual history. He has recently team-taught a seminar on history and film. He is the author of a monograph entitled *De Gaulle's France* (General Learning Press, 1973) and has published articles on French and Belgian political history in scholarly reviews. He has also written extensively on current political and cultural issues in *Commonweal* and other journals.

James Michael Welsh was born in Logansport, Indiana, and was educated at Indiana University and the University of Kansas, where he was a research fellow in analytical bibliography and served as chairman of the classical film series on campus. He currently teaches film and English at Salisbury State College in Maryland. He is co-founding editor of *Literature/Film Quarterly*, associate editor of the *Washington Review of the Arts*, and contributing editor of *American Classic Screen*. He is coauthor (with D. Heyward Brock of the University of Delaware) of *Ben Jonson: A Quadricentennial Bibliography* (Scarecrow Press, 1974) and (with John C. Tibbetts of the University of Kansas) of *His Majesty the American: The Cinema of Douglas Fairbanks, Sr.* (A. S. Barnes, 1977). In 1973 he hosted a television series, *The Films of the Gatsby Era*, produced by the Maryland Center for Public Broadcasting and aired on some twenty member stations of the Eastern Educational Network, from Boston to Miami.

Editor's Foreword

It is a particular pleasure to present as one of the earliest publications in this series a book about Abel Gance, for Gance exemplifies even more precisely than other great filmmakers the concept of *auteurism* underlying the design of this series. Over the course of sixty years, Gance—who is still active in 1977—has directed a great many films; but he wishes to be remembered for only a small number of them. Even more significantly, some of his most cherished projects remain unrealized.

Gance distinguishes—as the authors of this book point out—between the work that one does to live and that which one does "in order not to die." Gance regards the greater number of pictures that he has directed as assignments that he was compelled to accept for financial reasons and as ventures that failed to give him an opportunity to bring his personal vision to life on the screen. Although Gance recognized that filmmaking was a business and complied with the demands of producers insensitive to the artistic potential of the medium, he has steadfastly maintained that the motion picture was primarily an art form and that only those films that were inspired by an artist's vision were worth remembering and preserving.

The enormous cost of filmmaking presents an unparalleled problem to the artist who seeks to fulfill his vision through the cinema. There are examples in such other arts as painting and novel writing of artists who have had to accept commercial assignments in order to support themselves until they could get on with what they regarded as their really important work; but no other art form presents such massive financial problems as does the production and distribution of motion pictures. Yet the true art treasures of the screen—those works that we can place beside the great paintings and novels—are those few that a small company of visionaries have succeeded in creating despite the staggering problems of adequately financing

5

productions. Even many of these works—like Erich von Stroheim's *Greed* and Max Ophuls's *Lola Montes*—have suffered, after being completed, at the hands of producers and distributors motivated entirely by financial considerations and indifferent—if not actually hostile—to the artistic intentions of the *auteur*. Every great director has encountered obstacles that have forced him to compromise his vision, and the careers of some—like Orson Welles—have been almost entirely a succession of frustrating disappointments.

The concept behind this series of books is to seek out the relatively small number of motion pictures (and related art works) that have been primarily motivated by artistic considerations—whether the creator's vision has led to a work that is artistically successful or not—and to illuminate the story of their creation and the merits of what has been created. We do not contend that every production of even the most outstanding filmmakers is of individual interest. Critics do not judge F. Scott Fitzgerald by his Pat Hobby stories; yet some critics who are incomprehensibly hostile to auteurist criticism try to minimize the importance of the director in filmmaking because of the unevenness of the achievement of even some of the medium's greatest artists. Whatever the contributions of co-workers to the creation of a cinematic masterpiece, the director is finally responsible for the success of what we *see*. Bad acting, insensitive producing, awkward scriptwriting can ruin what might have become a successful film, but only a gifted director can transform the contributions of good actors, intelligent producers, and able writers into a memorable aesthetic experience. The wonder is not that there have been so few great films, but that some remarkable persons have on a few occasions directed the fusion of many components into a successful whole. Great art is never produced by a committee.

No one has discriminated more severely among his own works or has pleaded more urgently over a longer span of time for the chance to realize some of his most ambitious visions than Abel Gance. The authors of this book have correctly concentrated on those few of his visions that he has been able to realize in some form and those works that still remain only his private visions. Even the small body of work that Gance cherishes has been quite variously received by critics. The writers of this book are not his slavish admirers. What they realize, however, is that what is important about Gance is not his uninspired commercial ventures or even the sometimes excesses of his most cherished projects, but his unflagging vision of what the cinema might become.

Appreciation of Gance as a theorist and artist has unhappily been most difficult in the United States because of the unavailability of those works on which he must be judged. As the authors point out, only a single deteriorating print of *Beethoven* remains in this country; none is available of *Cyrano et d'Artagnan*. However Gance may finally be judged, those committed to the advancement of cinema as an art form must become familiar with his work.

Hopefully this book, setting forth what needs to be known about Abel Gance as theorist and artist, will be a first step toward the development of our understanding of this unique contributor to the emergence of the "seventh art." Once Gance becomes familiar to admirers of film as an art form, increased demand should help make his important work available. Already, as the authors report, some of his most ambitious projects, like the "Napoleon" film that has taken a number of different forms over the course of more than fifty years, are being restored for circulation. In his last years Gance may yet witness the understanding and appreciation of his work that he has long sought. We are proud to publish this sympathetic but unsentimental and exacting study of Gance as part of the long-overdue tribute that may win him the familiarity that he deserves among the pioneers in the development of the twentieth century's greatest contribution to the arts.

WARREN FRENCH

Preface

But who is Abel Gance? One should not have to raise such a question in these enlightened times when, more than ever before, serious attention is being directed toward the cinema; yet an artist is

9

known by his works, and Gance's works remain, for the most part,
unknown in this country. France knows and respects David Wark
Griffith, whose films can readily be seen there. Americans know
René Clair, Jean Vigo, Jean Renoir, and Marcel Carné; their work is
easily available here because it has received the necessary critical
attention. It is a mystery to us, however, why the work of Abel
Gance, who has been recognized as one of the founders of French
cinema and whose contributions in his native country match those of
Griffith in the United States and Eisenstein in the Soviet Union,
should have gone unnoticed for so many years in America. To be
sure, the situation is changing as Gance's films gradually are becoming available and beginning to attract the attention they deserve.
But the fact that Gance's epic *Napoléon*, for example, reached this
nation's capital nearly fifty years after its completion gives witness to
a central truth in the filmmaker's career: this gifted and visionary
artist and innovator has always operated far in advance of his times.

Some sixty years ago when the cinema was nothing more than a
form of popular entertainment, a small group of men, not all of them
in film, nor born to it, realized that motion pictures had tremendous
potential. Because cinema was an art, it could move men. These
people, as varied in their walks of life as Lenin and Robert Flaherty,
looked beyond what was being shown to the public on the screens of
their day and foresaw an art form so powerful it could provide the
basis for creating a new society. To D. W. Griffith, Sergei Eisenstein, and Abel Gance the cinema would never repudiate its base in
popular culture, but it would not continue exclusively as vulgar
entertainment. It would realize itself and become a vehicle for de-
termining the future. Among these great visionaries, Gance was a
leader by virtue of his informed idealism. He saw film as a com-
munal ceremony for the religion of the future. He was a kind of
prophet. He was recognized, but not followed.

The situation in the United States began to change in April of
1973 when Kevin Brownlow's reconstructed version of Gance's
Napoléon was shown at the American Film Institute Theater in
Washington's Kennedy Center. This rarely seen "complete" *Napoléon* had not been available in this country, nor anywhere else, since
its Paris premiere, mainly because of the demands it makes on
projection facilities—and it is only because of the dedicated labors of
Kevin Brownlow that a version of the original epic has been preserved and reassembled. As an entertainment vehicle, *Napoléon*
makes extreme demands: a five-hour film may understandably be

considered rather excessive; certainly that verdict was imposed upon von Stroheim's *Greed* in this country. But like *Greed*, Gance's *Napoléon* stands up as one of the truly remarkable monuments of the cinema. One wonders if there has ever been a film that could match its richness of visual metaphor, to say nothing of its technical innovations. Abel Gance combines the unique talents of the artist, the philosopher, and the inventor into one incredible personality. He had the technical skill to shape his medium so that it would better serve his artistic vision. He developed and patented the idea for what we now know as "Cinerama," which he utilized in the final portion of *Napoléon*, attempting to extend the visual boundaries of the cinema at a time when other innovators were attempting to develop the dimension of sound. And in the development of sound Gance was also a pioneer in his native country. Without question, then, *Napoléon* is a work of genius, but it is by no means the only film of merit Abel Gance has given us.

Abel Gance made six major films—*J'Accuse* (two versions: 1919 and 1938), *La Roue* (1921), *Napoléon* (1927), *Beethoven* (1936), *Cyrano et d'Artagnan* (1963)—and many lesser ones, "not to live," as he likes to say, "but in order not to die." At eighty-eight, Abel Gance has work in progress, work as yet unseen, and scripts for films not yet begun. Like the man himself, his work spans the period of film history from its days of early development shortly before the First World War to the present. Fifty years have elapsed since *Napoléon* was released. This film, and, indeed, all the others, has only been shown infrequently in this country, and not at all regularly in France. To be seen in its original state, *Napoléon* requires special screening facilities. *La Roue*, a masterpiece, is nearly unavailable in both countries. *Beethoven* and *Cyrano* have remained largely unknown in the United States, which means unseen. *J'Accuse* exists in a truncated 35 mm. version in the Film Collection of the Museum of Modern Art, but only in the 1938 sound version. The 1919 silent film version is not available here at all. And yet, with reason, the legend of Abel Gance persists, even in the United States.

Gance has been generously treated by those few who have written about him in English. Paul Rotha, in *The Film Till Now* considered Gance, on the evidence of his two biographical films (*Napoléon* and *Beethoven*), to be the only director "who has actually recreated the aura of greatness on the screen, and given some key to what it essentially is in a gifted individual." More recently, Kevin

Brownlow may be said to have "rediscovered" Gance for a later generation of viewers in his remarkable history of early film achievement, *The Parade's Gone By. . .* , a book dedicated to Abel Gance. Arthur Lennig's essays on *La Roue* and *Napoléon* in the *Persistence of Vision* anthology are intelligently written appreciations. Gance has fared less well at the hands of some influential French critics who none the less recognize the man's importance for the history of film. In *French Film*, for example, Georges Sadoul ridicules the "extreme and often exasperating romanticism" of *La Roue* and writes disparagingly of *Napoléon* as "third-rate or worse." Sadoul criticized *Napoléon* for what he took to be its unconscious caricature of "both Napoleon (of whom Gance was a great admirer) and the Revolution (which he abhorred)." Yet even Sadoul admitted that *Napoléon*, the film, contained "passages of almost epic force, the work of a master."

The most worthwhile and serious academic study of the director is Roger Icart's *Abel Gance* (1960). We believe it is appropriate, however, that one of the best introductions to the cinema of Abel Gance has come to this country not through the publishing trade, but through the cinema itself. Nelly Kaplan's documentary film *Abel Gance: Hier et demain* (1963) provides stunning evidence of Gance's talent by providing sequences from *La Roue*, *Napoléon*, and the rest of his major films. And Gance is there himself to tell us the story of his career. He explains his early literary and dramatic frame of mind: he tells us, for example, about his play, *The Victory of Samothrace*, that was to have starred Sarah Bernhardt, but which was never produced because of the advent of World War I, and one immediately recalls D. W. Griffith's early ambitions as a playwright. The film later shows a photograph of Abel Gance shaking hands with Mr. Griffith in New York, as Gance explains that during that meeting in the early 1920s each director realized that the other had independently "discovered" the use of the close-up. A few years later, just as Alfred Hitchcock made the first sound picture with dialogue in England *(Blackmail)*, so Abel Gance made the first sound picture with dialogue in France *(La Fin du Monde)*. Gance's inventions—Polyvision, Perspective Sound, and the Pictographe, for example—are all demonstrated in Nelly Kaplan's documentary, as is his later idea for "Magirama," which he attempted to put into practice during the 1950s—an attempt to utilize the spectacular potential of the cinema to overwhelm audiences, to enchant and stun them in a way that only the cinema can do. And in this respect the documentary makes clear that central "flaw" which has plagued Abel Gance throughout his career—the fact that this filmmaker's ideas were almost always years ahead of his times.

The other documentary, one which has just recently become available in the United States, is Kevin Brownlow's *The Charm of Dynamite*, a fifty-minute study that skillfully combines interviews with Gance and his collaborators with extensive clips from the 1919 *J'Accuse*, *La Roue*, and *Napoléon*, and behind-the-scenes footage to show how the epic *Napoléon* was made. The emphasis here on *Napoléon* is, of course, understandable, since Brownlow's work in reassembling that film, bringing it within a minute of its original running time, has rescued this "classic" for posterity. Most important, however, *The Charm of Dynamite* effectively conveys a sense of Gance's impressive personal magnetism.

Abel Gance is the epitome of what the cinema might have become but never did. No study of him will do justice to his beliefs or his films—and they are indistinguishable—by remaining rooted in film history or film criticism. We must look back to the Paris of the early twentieth century and attempt to place this filmmaker in his cultural and intellectual context. Gance must be seen in the company of that glorious pantheon of contemporaries of the first two decades of this century. Like Picasso, Braque, and Matisse, he responded to minds that were not themselves of his chosen field. Gance, like Griffith, Flaherty, René Clair, Buñuel, Eisenstein, and Dovzhenko, did not begin as a filmmaker. He began as an actor who then became a writer. His first work of art was a play. An early chapter of this book discusses, therefore, in some detail, the intellectual environment whence Gance emerged. We then move to a consideration of his most important films—*J'Accuse*, *La Roue*, *Napoléon*, and *Beethoven*—and conclude with an appreciation of one of his favorite unrealized projects, a life of Columbus, which is perhaps the one scenario most on his mind in his later years. Minor works undertaken for commercial reasons—the movies that caused some to regard him as the De Mille of France rather than the D. W. Griffith of Europe (in Kevin Brownlow's terms)—are mentioned only in passing but accounted for in an appended filmography.

In the preparation of this book we have translated many pages of Gance's theoretical writings and speculations about the cinema. Since hardly any of these primary sources have been available in English, we have taken the liberty of quoting him—extensively, from time to time—while attempting to preserve in translation at least some of the vitality and enthusiasm of his original words. Our treatment of Gance's play, *The Victory of Samothrace,* and of his "Columbus" scenario could not have been written without the director's willingness to lend us manuscript materials, since neither work has ever appeared in print. Thanks also to the filmmaker himself, his ideas in his advanced years are represented in this account, which ends with a transcript of a recent interview.

STEVEN P. KRAMER

JAMES M. WELSH

Acknowledgments

In the five years it has taken us to get this book into finished form, the authors have become indebted to a number of generous and helpful people. Among those we know who have read all or part of the manuscript are Ernest Callenbach, Gerald Mast, Richard Dyer MacCann, and Penelope Houston. We exonerate them from such flaws as the book may still contain and thank them for any encouragement they might have given us. Early in the project Marie Epstein of the Cinémathèque Française helped to make Gance materials available for study in France; also most helpful in this regard during the later stages were M. Claude Lafaye and Mlle. Isabelle Montagne of the Centre du Cinéma Français, without whose cooperation Gance's work on *Cyrano et d'Artagnan* could not have been covered here. Claude-Marie Senninger also gave invaluable assistance on *Cyrano*. In the United States, Robert Harris of Images Motion Picture Rental Library was especially helpful, as were Charles Silver of the Film Department at the Museum of Modern Art and Jean Donnelly, formerly of Cinema V. Herman Weinberg provided much help and cooperation regarding stills to illustrate the book. Christa Fehrer of *Literature/Film Quarterly* helped willingly with the proofreading.

A number of friends and colleagues read portions of the manuscript and provided helpful criticism—in particular, Larry Hirschorn of the University of Pennsylvania, Michael Friedmann of the University of Pittsburgh, and Jeremy Cott. We are especially grateful, however, to Richard C. Keenan of the University of Maryland, Eastern Shore, and to James Fasanelli of the University of Maryland, Baltimore County, who gave the entire manuscript a careful and sensitive reading and suggested a number of stylistic and structural emendations. But our greatest debt on this score is to Warren

15

French, who saw a book in what we finally offered him and generously helped to shape and publish it.

Portions of this book first appeared in earlier versions in the following periodicals and are reprinted here by permission: Chapter 9 ("Film As Incantation") in *Film Comment;* Chapter 6 ("Beethoven," expanded and revised) in *Sight and Sound;* and Chapter 3 ("Gance's Accusations Against War") in *Cinema Journal.* Our translation of Canudo's "Manifesto of the Seven Arts," extensively quoted in Chapter 2, first appeared in *Literature/Film Quarterly* and is used here by permission of the editors. Unless otherwise indicated, the stills that illustrate this book are from the collection of Herman G. Weinberg.

We should also like to acknowledge with gratitude plans currently underway to preserve archivally Gance's best work in cinema. The process begins with collecting, and Kevin Brownlow's work on *Napoléon* set an important precedent. In France, Henri Langlois was a redoubtable film collector, and his work at the Cinémathèque Française must be considered unique. The second step in the process, however, involves the transfer of nitrate materials to more permanent acetate stock, an expensive procedure and one that, because of the costs involved and the huge store of materials to be preserved, is not even adequately funded in the United States. In France, nitrate prints are stored at Bois d'Arcy, a former military fort near Paris. According to Gilbert Adair *(Film Comment,* vol. 13, no. 6, p. 3*)*, these nitrate prints "are being eaten up by humidity. No work of restoration or even supervision has been undertaken for twenty years." It would be pointless to speculate about the future of the Cinémathèque at present, but we hope that Gance materials in its keeping will eventually be carefully preserved for posterity.

In the United States, meanwhile, Images, the American distributor of Gance's films, is working with the Museum of Modern Art reconstructing a complete version of the sound *J'Accuse* 'from 35mm. master materials, a version that will run to about 123 minutes. All of the original uncut material will be held and archivally preserved by the Museum of Modern Art, and this same procedure will apply to all Gance films that Images distributes in this country. The most recent materials we know of as of this writing are 35mm. master fine grains of the fourteen-reel nitrate negative for the 1928 re-release version of *La Roue* and a 16mm. negative of *En Tournant La Roue,* recently located in a version owned by a private collector that runs to about twenty-five minutes. The point is, a Gance archive is now being developed in the United States through these measures, and that was not the case five years ago, when we began work on this book. We applaud the effort.

S. P. K.
J. M. W.

*   *   *

This book is dedicated
to our parents.

Chronology

1889   Abel Gance born in the XVIIIth *arrondissement* of Paris, October 25.

1897   Begins grammar-school education at Collège de Chantilly.

1901   Continues his education at Collège Chaptal in Paris.

1906   In deference to his father's wishes becomes a clerk in a solicitor's firm specializing in divorces; dislikes the work, but the experience gives him contact with real human problems.

1907   Disappoints and alienates his father by becoming an actor at the Théâtre du Parc in Brussels.

1908   Returns to Paris to continue his acting career.

1909   First experience as film actor in Léonce Perret's *Molière*. Begins writing scenarios—*Le Glas du Père Césaire* and *La Légende de l'Arc-en-ciel*—and is able to sell his work to Gaumont.

1910   Diagnosed as having tuberculosis; his health improves after recuperative period at the Casino de Vittel. Continues to write scenarios—*Paganini, La Fin de Paganini,* and *Le Crime de Grand-père* (for Louis Feuillade); *Le Roi des Parfums, L'Aluminite, L'Auberge rouge,* and *Un tragique amour de Mona Lisa* (for Albert Capellani).

1911   Returns to Paris, forms his own production company—Le Film Français—and directs his first film, *La Digue*, with Pierre Renoir. Continues writing scenarios: *Cyrano et D'Assoucy, Un Clair de lune sous Richelieu,* and *L'Electrocuté* (for Camille de Morlhon).

1912   Directs *Le Nègre blanc, Il y a des pieds au plafond,* and *Le Masque d'horreur,* all for Le Film Français.

1913   Returns to theater; writes his play *La Victoire de Samothrace,* but production plans are thwarted by the outbreak of World War I.

1914   When the war begins goes before seven boards of examiners
        before being demobilized. Resumes writing scenarios, but
        now for Louis Nalpas, new director of Le Film d'Art. Writes
        L'Infirmière (for Henri Pouctal), then begins directing his
        own films, the first, *Un Drame au Château d'Acre*, from his
        scenario entitled *Les Morts reviennent-ils?*

1915   Utilizes distorted images in *La Folie du Docteur Tube* and is
        criticized by Louis Nalpas for his experimentation. Begins to
        work on one of his many unrealized projects, "Ecce Homo."

1916   Continues experimenting in *Barberousse*, believed to con-
        tain the first close-up in French motion pictures; also intro-
        duces the horizontal wipe.

1917   Directs more conventional melodramas. In *Le Droit à la Vie*
        uses the close-up as a means of isolating and emphasizing
        actors. *Mater Dolorosa* is a great popular and commercial
        success. On September 27 is appointed artistic director of Le
        Film d'Art, but is soon to be mobilized into Service
        Cinématographique de l'Armée.

1918   Completes *La Dixième Symphonie*, an early melodramatic
        treatment of an artist. Falls in love with Ida Danis and di-
        vorces his first wife.

1919   Directs *J'Accuse*, a major statement concerning war. As
        Gance begins work on *La Roue*, Ida Danis is diagnosed as
        having an incurable case of pulmonary tuberculosis.

1921   *La Roue* marks a new advance in its experimental intercut-
        ting. Grief-stricken over the death of the woman he loves,
        Gance travels to America in summer and is introduced to
        D. W. Griffith in New York.

1923   Back in France directs *Au Secours!*, starring Max Linder.

1925   *Napoléon* project begins shooting at Billancourt Studios,
        January 17.

1926   On August 20 patents his wide-screen "Polyvision" triptych
        idea for use in *Napoléon;* this multiple-screen invention is a
        precursor of what, years later, is called "Cinerama."

1927   *Napoléon* premieres at the Paris Opéra on April 7.

1928   Begins work on another of his important unrealized projects,
        "Les Grands Initiés," intended to proclaim the ecumenicism
        of all world religions.

1929   Patents Perspective Sound on August 13. Lupu Pick's *Napo-
        léon à Sainte-Hélène*, with Werner Krauss in the title role,

produced from a Gance scenario that was originally part of the Napoleon project.

1930 Directs *La Fin du Monde*, the first French talking feature. Publishes *Prisme*.

1932 Patents Stereophonie, March 10. Makes a sound version of *Mater Dolorosa*.

1934 Completes the synchronized sound version of *Napoléon Bonaparte*.

1935 *Lucrèce Borgia*.

1936. *Beethoven* completed, with Harry Baur and Jean-Louis Barrault.

1937 Completes the sound version of *J'Accuse*, August 31. Begins work on "La Divine Tragédie," an unrealized project derived from the Christ episode of "Les Grands Initiés," planned as a Polyvision production.

1938 Patents Pictographe on August 1.

1939 Shooting scheduled to start June 12 on location in Granada for "Christophe Colomb." Work continues for thirty-five years on this, perhaps most important, of his unrealized projects.

1944 During the Occupation summoned to Germany to meet Hitler. Instead, flees to Spain and begins to film the uncompleted *Manolete* with Guerner as his cinematographer.

1954 *La Tour de Nesle* is a commercial success and serves to bring Gance back to public attention after a period of obscurity following the war. Writes scenario *La Reine Margot* for Jean Dreville. *Quatorze juillet*, an experimental short in color Polyvision and later included in *Magirama* premieres at the Gaumont-Palace, July 15.

1956 *Magirama* opens, an experimental program produced in collaboration with Nelly Kaplan, intended to demonstrate the potential of Polyvision, in part using sequences from his earlier films.

1959 Location shooting begins in Yugoslavia for *Austerlitz*, in CinemaScope and color, scripted in collaboration with Nelly Kaplan and released the following year.

1963 *Cyrano et d'Artagnan*.

1972 *Bonaparte et la Révolution*, produced in collaboration with Claude Lelouch.

1

The Birth of a *Cinéaste*

AS EARLY AS 1912, he saw the cinema as an art, but an art which remained undeveloped. Like tragedy at the time of Hardy, it awaited its Corneille, its first classic. Abel Gance envisioned an art "More simply grandiose and human, without being to cinematography what the last fifty years have been to literature. To innovate, not to follow that blubbering sentimentality or that mechanical comedy which seems fashionable only because the real route has not yet been traced. Above all, not to do theatre, but to create allegory and symbol; to seize the basis of each civilization, to construct the admirable scenario which characterizes it, to embrace all the cycles of all the epics in succession, I repeat, to have this cinematographic classic which shall orient cinema to a new era. That's part of my great dream." Even so early in his career as filmmaker, Gance sensed his own potential for achieving this dream: "Soon a day will come, I hope, when my ramblings shall become tangible and shall show what can be hoped from this admirable synthesis of the movement of space and time."[1]

Abel Gance was born in Paris on October 25, 1889, the son of Adolphe and Françoise Perthon Gance. He was educated first at the Collège du Chantilly, then, after 1901, at Collège Chaptal in Paris. Although he was a good student with a voracious appetite for literature, poetry, and drama, Gance apparently disliked boarding school; but his interest in writing and his creative temperament led to his producing the class newspaper.[2] The young Abel Gance looked forward to a career in the arts, but his father, a practical man, wanted him to become a notary or a lawyer. According to Kevin Brownlow, Gance's father's attitude toward the arts "mirrored that of many Victorians, involved in what they considered more essential work, for whom painting, writing, and acting were not occupations so much as immoral frivolity."[3] Therefore, when he was seventeen

The daring distortion of images in La Folie ᵈᵘ Dr. Tube *(1915).*

years old, at the urging of his father Gance was put to work as a clerk
in a solicitor's office specializing in divorce cases. Although the experience gave him some useful exposure to human problems beyond his existing range of experience, Gance was not happy in this
employment. At the age of eighteen, against his father's wishes, he
decided to abandon it and try his fortune as an actor at the Théâtre
du Parc in Brussels.

This decision caused a serious estrangement between Gance and
his father; but it also gave the young man an opportunity to develop
as an artist and to meet other people of similar interests. After a
fairly successful first year as an actor at the Théâtre du Parc, Gance
returned to Paris when his contract had expired in 1908 and soon
made friends with a widening circle of talented people, including
Blaise Cendrars, Léger, Apollinaire, Canudo, Catulle Mendès,
Delaunay, Marinetti, Chagall, Sèverin-Mars, Pierre Magnier, Val-
land, and others. By 1909—the same year he made his debut as a
film actor in Léonce Perret's *Molière*—Gance was writing scenarios
which he was able to sell to Gaumont for money; even so, it was not
until later that he would develop a serious interest in the film as an
art. At first, it was merely a living: "When I began writing
scenarios," Gance recalled to Kevin Brownlow, "I decided to sell
them to Gaumont. I wrote a dozen or so small scenarios—four or
five pages—and sold them for fifty to a hundred francs. . . . You
could eat for three days on fifty francs, that was all."[4]

In 1910 Gance was diagnosed as having tuberculosis; consequently, he managed to get a contract at the Casino de Vittel, in
an area supposed to be good for health. Gance astonished his doc-
tors by treating himself successfully, away from the polluted air of
Paris. By 1911 his health had improved sufficiently to enable his
return to Paris, where he then formed his own production company
and made his first film—*La Digue*, with Pierre Renoir, the brother
of Jean Renoir.[5]

By 1917, he had made over a dozen films, essentially
melodramas. For the most part, however, these were commercial
products, films that were made for money. They enabled the young
Gance to concentrate on his real concerns—poetry, theater, and the
study of philosophy. These early film do not reveal the inner
workings of Gance's mind. In order to understand Gance's interior
development during these years before he had fully accepted the
cinema as his proper vehicle for artistic expression, we must turn to

his major play, *La Victoire de Samothrace*, written between September 1912 and June 1913.

La Victoire de Samothrace, Gance's first ambitious work, reveals how much its author was affected both by the extreme romanticism of his time and by the tradition of classical Greek theater.[6] This play may be considered especially important because it is the true forerunner of Gance's major films. Its heroine, Hellé, is the sister of Jean Diaz and Novalic, the heroes of *J'Accuse* and *La Fin du Monde*, but the play foreshadows thematic concerns as well. Written in what Gance considered an age of decadence about an age of decadence, *La Victoire* proposes to show how mankind may make a spiritual breakthrough and how art can assist in this process. In order to prove this point, the play breaks decisively with French classical theater.

La Victoire de Samothrace takes a classical situation and evolves a solution which transcends the classical solution. The argument at the opening might come straight out of Corneille: Hellé, daughter of Antigone, Prince of Syria, is the lover of Meneleas, brother of Ptolemy, Satrap of Egypt. Since these two princes are at war, one expects to be confronted with the usual choice between love and honor. But Gance is not concerned with honor, a value of the social community, but with spirituality, with man's relationship to the divine. Hellé's solution of the dilemma transcends her sense of duty and her feelings. She becomes the agent of a spiritual change which will transform the very grounds of existence.

Hellé feels the power to become more than a woman. As one other character says to her: "Great sister! You are not like the others. Love doesn't tarnish the marble. . . . You seem to bear the future in your hands!" To which Hellé replies: "I need to be a light in the light . . . I must not die because I feel that all the love of a generation of men would not suffice to satiate my force of giving. I love my Beauty more than Meneleas adores me. That's why, you see, I didn't kill myself, because I dedicate myself to a life greater than love!" Hellé is jealous of statues.

For Hellé to attain divinity, she needs an artist to immortalize her. Praxiteles, who is attempting to sculpt her, is "used up, sunk in the luxury of the Egyptian court." He seems to have abdicated his genius. The statue he is making of her "gives the impression of a disturbing hermaphroditism. It shows the decline of a genius who didn't have the strength to rise up, and whom Asiatic exoticism

perverted." Like the other Greeks of the Hellenistic age, he no
longer has a fatherland. Praxiteles calls upon Hellé to help him to
resurrect his art: "To make a cry of Victory, a song of stone which
the centuries will learn. . . . To make of granite a light more lumi-
nous than light, a woman more beautiful than life. . . . To make the
Work which will put an end to discords. . . . To create, to create, to
create!"

But Praxiteles has not suffered enough. He asks Hellé to call him
at the "great day of suffering." On the eve of the impending battle,
Hellé leaves the island where Meneleas is encamped to go to
Athens. She wants to prevent war, to eliminate the possibility of
seeing her lover killed by her brother.

The battle is supposed to be decided by single combat of two
ships. Hellé manages to get on her brother's ship. She dresses
herself in the wings of Eros stolen from the temple, and mounts a
lengthened cross on which the Greek and Syrian oriflammes are
attached. When Meneleas sees her, he calls on his men not to shoot.
Hellé declaims:

> In the name of Sacred Art awakening in my hand,
> Do not impede the instant which tomorrow shall be God
> If you allow my pure self, which enrages you, to inspire you.
> Do not impede the instant which shall greaten the world,
> For I shall remain, wandering the seas,
> Tied to this stem post, with my luminous gesture!
> Glories, Sorrows shall drink at my breasts,
> And mad artists shall hang on my wings!
> They shall call me Dream. . . Inspirer . . . Hope . . .
> and Myth . . . and Folly . . . and they shall come to see me!
>
> *Praxiteles*
> Do not blind yourself to deny the light! . . .
>
> *Hellé*
> Each century needs a great gesture to illuminate it—
> Even if bought at the price of a people,
> Let it be the flight of Hellé, the groping of Hellé.
> If I have vanquished love, it's to await the day
> When a more beautiful century wants another light,
> To stanch the thirst of more beautiful lovers.
> I live awaiting the birth of other Gods

> And shall abandon the pillory of my dreams
> If the marble begins where my gesture ends!
> Others perhaps one day on other crosses shall come.
> Bend to my voice! As yet, I am alone.

But Praxiteles is not yet prepared to immortalize her: "I believed in the instant of passion /I believed that it would suffice to have seen her to create." Meneleas's soldiers, furious at having lost Egypt for a vain hope, force him to execute his children, and seek sensual satisfaction by raping the courtesan Lamia, whom Hellé had once rescued from destruction at their hands.

In the fourth act, Meneleas's boat is covered with the phantasmagoric red light of the lighthouse. The boat is burning. Meneleas attaches Hellé to the Egyptian cross in the hope of saving her. Now she calls on Praxiteles—the beauty of her death transcends that of her life. Having accomplished her mission, she can now admit to her feelings as a woman, to her doomed love for Meneleas:

> Who shall pursue my deed further towards the day?
> Who shall be able, freely like me
> Not know how to die when death is so sweet
> Not know how to live without dying of love?

In typical romantic fashion, Eros finds consummation in Thanatos.

In the fifth act, Praxiteles has a nightmare that his statue doesn't really resemble Hellé. He demands of the gods the right to compare his statue with the model. Hellé appears; all the great sculptors cry out their admiration. Praxiteles denies that he deserves credit: his hands merely followed a strange light. Praxiteles asks that the authorship of the statue never be revealed. He enters a cavern. As if coming from the bowels of the earth, one hears his words: "The wheat does not know the name of him who sows!" Praxiteles dies; "sacred music and the voice of the sea seem to accompany the soul of the sculptor which rises in the Victory."

La Victoire de Samothrace foreshadows much of what Gance will do later in his films. Triumph lies not in material success, but in an artistic transcendence of the material world. One senses that Gance's ideas for an alternative art form are already fully developed and that all that is required are the means to expound them. The play is in a sense antitheater. It is more an oratorio than a drama.

There is little action or character analysis. Although it retains the traditional division into five acts and uses *alexandrins* in important places, it is the very antithesis of seventeenth-century theater. Through the use of tableaux, music, lighting, Gance evokes a religious mood.

Gance's friend the art historian Elie Faure disliked the theater because he felt that it epitomized the anomic and atomic quality of modern society. Gance's play is the very opposite of the kind of theater which Faure abhorred. This play is mystical and metaphysical rather than analytical and social or psychological. It seems clear that Gance, an avid student of Nietzsche, was influenced by *The Birth of Tragedy*. Nietzsche there argues that the decline of Greek culture was related to the disintegrative influence of the Socratic scientific spirit, which destroyed the coexistence of Apollonian and Dionysian principles within the tragedy. Tragedy was replaced by comedy, the Greek lost his unity with the cosmic forces surrounding him. Nietzsche believed that some day the scientific spirit would come to the realization that science could not resolve all the mysteries of life, and a sense of the tragic would return. *La Victoire de Samothrace* and Gance's subsequent films can be seen as an attempt to replace melodrama with tragedy in order to restore the sense of the tragic described by Nietzsche:

Like a mighty titan, the tragic hero shoulders the whole Dionysiac world and removes the burden from us. At the same time, tragic myth, through the figure of the hero, delivers us from our avid thirst for earthly existence and reminds us of another existence and a higher delight. For this delight the hero readies himself, not through his victories, but through his undoing. Tragedy interposes a noble parable, *myth*, between the universality of its music and the Dionysiac disposition of the spectator and in so doing creates the illusion that music is but a supreme instrument for bringing to life the plastic world of myth. [7]

La Victoire de Samothrace was never performed or even published. The young Gance had offered the play to Sarah Bernhardt, who agreed to act in it. The outbreak of World War I, however, made the performance impossible. If this play had been successfully produced, might Gance have remained a playwright? The suggestion is intriguing, yet one wonders nonetheless whether Gance was not destined for the cinema. For in March 1912, when Gance wrote about film, he described it as a "sixth art in which beat the wings of the Victory of Samothrace."[8] Perhaps this play was already his preparation for the cinema. At any rate, Gance's flirtation with the theater was to be short-lived and unfulfilled. The theories of his artistic comrades had stressed the limitations of the theater in favor of the cinema, and one suspects that Gance, influenced both by his friends and his experience, was naturally propelled not toward the proscenium arch, but toward the magic lantern. A few years later Sergei Eisenstein would turn to cinema after a period of intense and frustrating theatrical experimentation. But it was not until 1920 that Eisenstein joined the Proletkult Theatre in Moscow. Several years before this, in Paris, Abel Gance was already learning the craft of cinematography.

By 1915 Gance had produced a little comedy which foreshadowed far greater things. *La Folie du Docteur Tube,* starring Albert Dieudonné (later to play the role of Napoleon), was a farce about a mad scientist with a crazily misshapen head, who discovers a sneezing powder which has the power to change people's shapes. He utilizes this powder on two women, and then on their fiancés. The experience ends on a note of good humor, with the couples returning to their normal shapes, and taking a glass of champagne with the doctor. Tube then tries to stick his head into a bird cage. What is significant about this film is not the story, but the use of mirrors to distort shapes and motion. Because this is perhaps the first extensive use of distortion, many people consider that the film marks the appearance of the avant-garde in French cinema.

What Gance attempted in *Docteur Tube* was no doubt too advanced, too daring, too experimental. The film was not commercially successful; the Film d'Art executives were displeased. Gance's other films of this period were profitable, however, and by 1917 the filmmaker was more firmly established in the Film d'Art organization than ever, as evidenced by the following passage from *Prisme* (a book Gance published in 1930, compiled from his earlier notebooks and journals): "On September 27, 1917, I am offered the artistic direction of the Film d'Art. I would not note this fact in my journal if it weren't going to have a rather large influence on my future. Am I not going to divert what remains of my energies in trying to teach everyone a language which I barely know how to stammer myself?"[9]

Yet despite his misgivings, Gance now had the security and where-
withal necessary to advance his ideas about the cinema as art and to
put them into practice.

Consequently, in 1917 Louis Nalpas of Film d'Art gave Gance
40,000 francs and a *carte blanche* to make a serious film. The result
was *Mater Dolorosa*, a film of real artistic quality, yet one which
remains within the general melodramatic framework. *Mater
Dolorosa* displays a highly developed sense of composition. Gance
has by now discovered, for example, the use of contrasts which
proves so effective in his later films—a dark figure against a lumi-
nous and opaque window, the use of veils or grilles to produce a
mottled surface. At certain moments, the face of Dr. Berliac in
Mater Dolorosa approaches the agony of Sisif, the central character
of the later masterpiece *La Roue*. Nonetheless, the acting remains
overly theatrical, and little cutting is used to relieve the monotony
of the fixed camera. There are some very moving scenes, however,
like the one in which Berliac picks up the lace veil of the wife he
thinks has betrayed him.

La Dixième Symphonie, completed in 1918, struggles even more
valiantly than *Mater Dolorosa* against the constraints of the melodramatic structure. In an address entitled "La Beauté à travers le
cinéma," written for the Institut Général Psychologique and published in 1926, Gance posed the following question, then answered
it: "What does cinema need to be richer? Suffering. She is young;
she has not wept. Few men have died of her, by her, for her. Genius
works in the shadow of sadness until shadow becomes light again.
Cinema doesn't have shadows of that sort, and that's why it has not
yet had great artists."[10] *La Dixième Symponie* concerns an artist who
works in the "the shadow of sadness." Kevin Brownlow discloses
that Gance's inspiration for this picture came from Berlioz, who
once proclaimed: "I am about to start a great symphony in which my
great sufferings will be portrayed." Brownlow's own summary of the
action, however, leaves little doubt about the nature of the plot:

Eve Dinant (Emmy Lynn) marries Enric Damor, a composer (Séverin-
Mars), who is a widower with one child, Claire, of marriageable age (Mlle.
Nizan). Eve has not told Damor of her past, for while attempting to free
herself from a former lover, Frederic Ryce (Jean Toulout), she accidentally
killed his sister. Since that day, Ryce has blackmailed her; when he begins
courting Claire, Eve tries to stop the marriage, but she cannot produce a
satisfactory reason. Damor is deeply hurt, and accuses her of being in love

with Ryce herself. . . . Eve is ready to sacrifice her own happiness and return to Ryce, if he will only leave Claire alone. Eventually, Damor discovers the truth and forgives his wife.[11]

Into this situation so typical of melodrama, in which the question of fidelity poses itself as the primary concern, Gance attempts to thrust the problem of artistic creation. In asserting that "melodrama is a misleading description for films such as this," Brownlow perhaps confuses potential with accomplishment, which is easily enough done if the secondary concern of *Le Dixiéme Symphonie* be stressed over the obviously primary one. The doubting husband is also a composer, whose musical idol is Beethoven. When he performs his new symphony on the piano before an audience, through his suffering he is virtually transformed into Beethoven. And as he becomes Beethoven, his symphony becomes the "Tenth Symphony," the symphony that Beethoven might have composed, had he lived longer. This attempt to make a serious statement, however, is at odds with the sentimental plot. Gance tries to transfigure the old genre by injecting a higher meaning, but it is the higher meaning which, ultimately, is lost.

La Dixième Symphonie possesses many of the attributes which would make Gance's later films outstanding; but they are not fully realized here. The plot, centered around marital fidelity, seems a mere pretext for expressing some of Gance's deepest ideas; it is simply too insignificant a vehicle to do so convincingly. But if *La Dixième Symphonie* is a failure, it is a failure which lights the way to future successes.

The film interestingly reflects some of Gance's perennial concerns. At the outset the heroine, played by Emmy Lynn, is juxtaposed with an image of the Victory of Samothrace. Like Hellé, she is destined to attain grandeur through suffering. Her husband, the composer Damor, portrayed by the great actor Séverin-Mars (whom Gance would also use in *J'Accuse* and *La Roue*), marks Gance's first cinematic involvement with the Beethoven theme. Finally, behind the ostensible plot lies another, less visible theme—that of a nightmare which weighs upon two individuals, but one from which they are finally able to escape. The problem of how to transcend forces beyond our control is posed in all of Gance's great films, especially in *La Roue* and *Beethoven*, and this theme most certainly is anticipated in *La Dixième Symphonie*.

By the time he made *La Dixième Symphonie*, Gance had mas-

tered the cinematic art as it was then practiced. Technically, his film
has many admirable qualities: its visual rhythms, its effective use of
composition and contrast, its alternating use of indoor and outdoor
shots. Good as it may be, however, the dramatic potential of this
film is not yet fully actualized. Though technically at ease in his new
medium, Gance is still not quite artistically at ease. Though he has
demonstrated a facility for making crowd-pleasing movies, he has
not yet established himself as a major talent. Then, suddenly, between *La Dixième Symphonie* and *J'Accuse*, only a matter of months,
a miracle seems to take place: a *cinéaste* and a cinematic art are born
in France.

Disrobing scene from *Lucrèce Borgia* (1935), demonstrating what Herman Weinberg has called Gance's "traditional French appreciation of Feminine pulchritude."

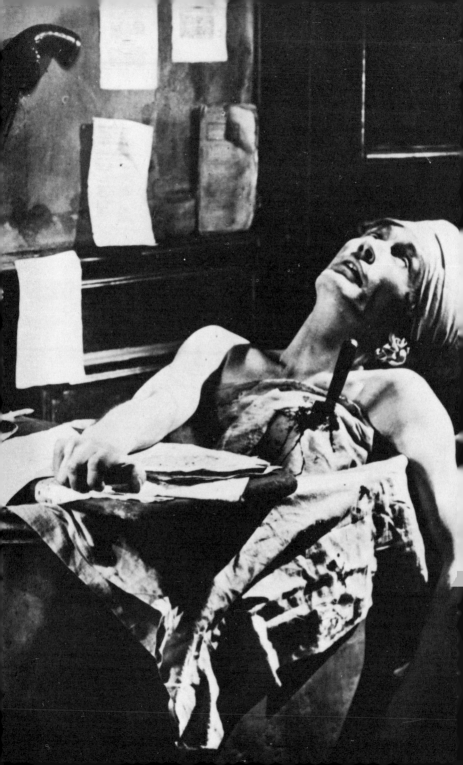

2

The Birth of the Seventh Art

ABEL GANCE may properly be considered a neglected artist and thinker. Before proceeding to discuss his major creations, we must, therefore, examine the reasons for that neglect, consider the man's alleged eccentricity, and demonstrate that, although some of the ideas that interested him may today seem peculiar he was never far removed from the main currents of intellectual speculation in France at the turn of the century. Because of Gance's passionate involvement with ideas and with the cinema, one might be tempted to view him as a sort of maniac who also happened to be a superb technician; to be sure, his genius has been fueled with maniacal energy. And, indeed, some of his beliefs may seem odd to us. But part of the difficulty may be that we cannot see the world and its problems from any kind of perspective that can approximate the situation of artistically inclined intellectuals in Paris over a half-century ago. Coming to maturity in the years preceding the First World War, Gance shares many of the intellectual tendencies of that generation, for his temperament was molded by that generation's frustrations and concerns.

Each age has its own way of thinking, its own vision of the natural and human world, its own "climate of opinion." Once we penetrate the minds of other periods, we are naturally struck by the strangeness of their point of view. The great debates of past ages often seem irrelevant and unreal to us, not because the answers appear clear from our vantage point, but because the very questions at debate seem irrelevant to us. As Carl Becker has explained: "Whether arguments command assent or not depends less upon the logic that conveys them than upon the climate of opinion in which they are sustained."[1] What we discover is that each age shares certain common grounds of debate. The debates of the medieval schoolmen, for example, have little meaning to our own way of thinking. The

35

medieval schoolmen may have been split between Nominalists and Realists, but these irreconcilable opponents shared certain basic postulates. Their debate makes no sense to us because our age no longer accepts those postulates.

What is true of the Middle Ages is equally true of later periods. The nineteenth century is in some ways, intellectually and chronologically, for example, so close to our times that we are apt to think that our perspective is relatively similar. In fact, the differences are greater than we think and difficult to perceive because of their superficial similarity. To understand fully even the men of the last century, we must attempt to come to terms with their points of view.

In our own century a tendency has developed to dismiss philosophical or metaphysical ideas as peculiar: "the essential quality of the modern climate of opinion," according to Carl Becker, "is factual rather than rational. The atmosphere which sustains our thought is so saturated with the actual that we can easily do with a minimum of the theoretical. . . . So long as we can make efficient use of things, we feel no irresistible need to understand them. No doubt it is for this reason chiefly that the modern mind can be so wonderfully at ease in a mysterious universe."[2]

This factual approach to ideas is reflected in the kind of neopositivist criticism recently so prevalent. It dismisses as "metaphysical" what it cannot analyze by its own, increasingly quantitative methodology. The discovery that a thinker's work is based on metaphysical principles may call into question the value of his ideas. The basic role of criticism, however, is to explain, not to "explain away." This means that criticism must see things in historical terms, must attempt to understand an artist or writer by establishing him in his historical context, listening sympathetically to what the man himself was trying to say and viewing understandingly what he tried to do.

In the discussion that follows, we will briefly examine the state of cinematic theory and practice in the years between 1911—the date of Ricciotto Canudo's seminal "Manifesto of the Seven Arts"—and the end of World War I. We will then look at the state of the French cinema, emphasizing in detail the theoretical contributions of the artists and critics in Gance's circle—in particular, Canudo, Elie Faure, and Jean Epstein.

In America at the time under scrutiny, D. W. Griffith had perfected his development of parallel montage toward melodramatic ends in *The Birth of a Nation* in 1915 and had then put the technique to thematic use in *Intolerance*. In the north of Europe Stiller and Sjöstrom had effectively photographed natural backgrounds to create an emotional ambience, and before 1920 Sjöstrom had experimented with depicting the supernatural in *The Phantom Carriage*. In Germany, *The Cabinet of Dr. Caligari* had dared to present "reality" through the deranged perceptions of an inmate of an insane asylum. The Soviets had not yet achieved their contribution in response to Lenin's charge that the illiterate masses be informed and taught through the universal language of the cinema. By the early 1920s, Kuleshov was at work on his montage experiments; Dziga Vertov, meanwhile, was working out his theories of *Kino Pravda*. Eisenstein would not make *Strike* until 1924, however, and *Potemkin* would not appear until the following year. In France, Abel Gance had already made parallel discoveries to those of Griffith, and his experiments on the editing table in *J'Accuse* and *La Roue*, later to be matched and multiplied in *Napoléon*, were—though not directed toward a common end—well in advance of Eisenstein.

Film historians outside of France have, by and large, paid minimal attention to the central developments of French cinema. They commonly discuss the work before 1910 of Méliès and the Lumière brothers, who conveniently took opposing positions between the documentary and more imaginative though less "realistic" approaches to filmmaking. But one is led to conclude that little or nothing of interest or significance happened in France between these very early pioneers and the likes of René Clair, Jean Vigo, and Jean Renoir in the 1930s. Actually, a great deal happened during this period.

One of the key developments was the Film d'Art movement, starting about 1908 with *L'Assassinat du duc de Guise*. The intention here was to formulate an entertaining medium that would present theatrical talents through the motion picture. Well-known actors and directors dominated the movement:

The Society of the Film d'Art brought its first love, the theatre, with it and all too easily fell into the set clichés first perpetrated by Méliès: its films were theatre in celluloid, every scene was shot straight through, from the same camera position, and simply presented the resulting series of images with no attempt to edit sequences.[3]

The major film directors who emerged from the war reacted against this tradition. Georges Sadoul describes the reaction of a group of

Impressionist filmmakers, led by Louis Delluc and including, with Gance, Marcel L'Herbier, Germaine Dulac, and Jean Epstein. Louis Delluc articulated their reaction to the Film d'Art movement: "The French cinema must be *cinema;* the French cinema must be *French,*" and the Impressionists asserted that film was "an art in its own right, having its own laws which must differentiate it from the other arts, and from literature and the theatre in particular."[4] Abel Gance shared these reservations, even though he had worked within the confines of the Society of the Film d'Art when making *Mater Dolorosa* in 1918.

Delluc and L'Herbier were both critical of the Film d'Art, although in other respects they differed artistically and temperamentally. L'Herbier was a formalist and, as an Impressionist, wanted to explore subjective reality. Delluc insisted that original scripts be written for the cinema. Out of this "new wave" also emerged an interest in experimental film, an avant-garde tendency that eventually led to the achievements of Jean Epstein and Germaine Dulac. This same experimental tendency is also demonstrated, of course, in the best work of Abel Gance.

At least equally as important to Gance's development as these cinematic movements is the intellectual atmosphere which nourished the ideas which he and others—Jean Epstein in particular —attempted to translate into visual and cinematic terms. Many writers and artists of this period were in revolt against the conventions and ideologies of bourgeois society, against hypocritical morality, and against materialism. They were also revolting against the scientific conception of the universe that was then in vogue, a universe that allowed no place for uncertainty. There was absolute Time and Place, just as there was Right and Wrong. The cosmos was seen in materialistic terms: Man had separated himself from Nature. Through the Industrial Revolution man had become a creature of artificial rather than natural rhythms. This "stifling" atmosphere led to the desire to escape and revolt.

Because of the equation of Mechanistic Physics and Science, or bourgeois morality and morality *per se,* the poet was likely to become irrational and amoral. The poet's experiences found no place in the "rational" universe. He had to go beyond Good and Evil, beyond Science. For this reason, artists and poets often joined those perennial underground movements which waged war against the mechanistic universe (such as Swedenborgianism, theosophy, astrology, occultism).

The scientific age had minimized the function of the poet. The poet had once been the *vates*, the seer, able to look into the mystery of things. Like priest or oracle, he was able to use his arcane powers to bring back Truth to ordinary mortals. Plato developed the idea of poetic fury *("furor poeticus")*, and said that the best things come from "madness." But, as J. W. N. Sullivan points out: "The materialistic doctrine that has most influenced aesthetic theory is the doctrine that the artist's perceptions give us no knowledge of the nature of reality."[5] The poet, then, would have no right to promise us the "New Heaven and the New Earth." The poet was reduced to being no more than the purveyor of minor sensual pleasures.

In a sense, the spiritual revolt of the artist found its parallel in developments within the world of science. Einstein with the theory of Relativity and Heisenberg with the Uncertainty Principle displaced Newton's mechanistic view of the universe; Freud's discovery of the unconscious shattered the rationalist psychologies of Locke and Condillac; Marxists and other radicals challenged the material predominance of the triumphant bourgeoisie. The possibility of a creative synthesis of all these elements was always there, though rarely and momentarily realized. The surrealists, for example, assimilated Freudian notions and joined hands, at least temporarily, with the Communist party. This is hardly to say that Marxism, Freudianism, and mysticism can be equated. Although they shared a common opposition to Establishment ideas, mysticism can be seen as a reaction against industrial and scientific trends, whereas Marx and Freud were responding to them.

Paris was the center of the cultural world of the late nineteenth and early twentieth century. It was the birthplace of countless artistic movements. In this turbulent atmosphere a group of men reached the conclusion that cinema was more than a form of cheap, commercial entertainment and bastardized melodrama. They defined film as the "Seventh Art"; the films they called for and produced are in large part related to the cultural atmosphere of their environment. Who were these men? What was their conception of the cinema?

The term "Seventh Art," as it emerged in the second decade of the twentieth century, was not the anodyne expression which it has since become. On the contrary, it was then a rallying-cry for a very distinct view of cinema as the instrument of a profound spiritual renovation of mankind. The term was invented by Ricciotto Canudo. The same conception was shared by the art historian Elie Faure, the *cinéaste* and critic Jean Epstein, and Abel Gance. All these were fiercely independent men. They did not constitute an organized movement; yet objectively, it is apparent that they shared the same basic conception of the role of film, and were considerably influenced by each other's ideas. Viewed from the outside, retrospectively, they can be seen to constitute a distinct school.

In general, these men believed that the world had reached the end of an age of anarchic and anomic individualism—an age symbolized by the theater. The Romantics had earlier idealized the Middle Ages, which they admired for the organic solidarity that unified church, state, and society. These theorists of the cinema envisioned the advent of a new age which would mean a return to organic solidarity, but on a higher plane than that of the Middle Ages. It would be based on the marriage of the Machine and Feeling. This society would require a new religion, mystic and vitalist in nature. The Cinema, the Seventh Art, would be the vehicle for propagating the new faith. But if cinema was to be the new language, its grammar had to be discovered and its vocabulary developed. It was to this task that these men set themselves.

The first aesthetician of the Seventh Art, Ricciotto Canudo, was born in Gioia del Colle (Bari) in 1877.[6] After studies in Florence and Rome and participation in intellectual circles (which comprised the writers and critics Papini and Prezzolini and the nationalist poet Corradini), Canudo came to Paris in 1902. This *"Barisien très Parisien,"* as he was nicknamed by his friend Apollinaire, threw himself into the world of the arts. In a manifesto of 1905 coauthored by A. Tudesq, Canudo called for a profound renewal of the arts and society. Canudo was involved in many movements and confined to none; with seemingly boundless energy he wrote poetry, published novels (inventing a style stressing interpersonal psychology, which he called *sinestismo*), created open-air theater in southern France. As an art critic, he discovered Chagall and organized a Chagall show in 1914. In that same year, together with Blaise Cendrars, he wrote an appeal for foreigners living in France to volunteer for the French army. Canudo was one of the 80,000 foreigners who enlisted.

Canudo's most significant role was that of journalist and editor. In 1913 he founded *Montjoie,* a rallying point at the time of the "battle" of Stravinsky's *Rite of Spring*. Started as a journal of "French cultural imperialism" intended to give direction to the artistic elite, it became the voice for "cerebralist art" (Canudo wrote the "Cerebralist Manifesto" in February 1914). In 1922 Canudo founded the *Gazette des Sept Arts*. This review, together with the Club of Friends of the Seventh Art, was meant to bring poets, painters, architects, and musicians together with the filmmakers.[7]

Jean Epstein describes Canudo's contribution to the development of film this way:

As early as 1911, Canudo published an essay on cinema which one can't re-read today without being overwhelmed by so much foresight. While for years to come, both in fact and in theory, film was to be nothing more than a distraction for adolescent outings, a sufficiently dark trysting-place, or a rather somnambulist trick of physics, Canudo had understood that cinematography could and should be a marvelous instrument of lyricism. He foresaw immediately the limits and the infinities of this new lyricism which didn't yet exist. . . .

Canudo was the first to think of showing the public selected film sequences at the Salon d'Automne, to constitute an anthology of cinema. The idea of a cinematographical anthology was extremely useful, because it attracted attention to the cinematic style itself. It isolated style from anecdote.[8]

For Abel Gance, Canudo was the prophet as well as the poet of the cinema.

The essence of Canudo's thought on film is contained in the "Manifesto of the Seven Arts" of 1911, which begins defiantly:

If the numberless and nefarious shopkeepers believed that they could raise the value of their industry and their commerce by appropriating the term "Seventh Art," they didn't accept the responsibility imposed by the word "Art." Their industry remains the same, more or less well organized from a technical point of view; their commerce is either flourishing or mediocre, depending on the rise and fall of universal emotivity; their "art," except in certain cases where the filmmaker wishes to impose his will and knows how to do it, remains pretty much that which animated Xavier de Montépin and the likes of Descourcelles. But that Art of total synthesis which is the cinema, that fabulous newborn progeny of the Machine and Feeling, begins to cease its wailings and enters into childhood. Its adolescence will soon come to seize its intelligence and multiply its dreams. We want to speed up its blossoming, to hasten the coming of its youth. *We need the Cinema to create the total art towards which the other arts, since the beginning, have always tended.*

Canudo goes on to summarize his understanding of the history
and purpose of art. Art had been created to affirm the "eternity of
things which move man," to enable men to rise above their own
selves. The two fundamental arts, architecture and music, had developed in opposite directions. Architecture, born of man's need for
shelter, soon individualized itself as did its complements, sculpture
and painting. Music, on the other hand, attempted to grasp the
"rhythms which govern all nature," and became increasingly
abstract, liberating itself from poetry and dance to become the pure
music of the symphony. Cinema finally closed the circle, making a
fusion of the plastic and rhythmic arts possible:

Today the "circle in movement" of aesthetics finally closes triumphantly on
that total fusion of art called Cinematography. If we take the ellipse as the
perfect geometric image of life, that is to say, of movement—of the movement of our sphere flattened at the poles—and if we project it on a horizon-
tal plane of paper, art, all art, appears thus:

Hundreds of human centuries have thrown into this ellipse in motion
their highest aspirations, always constructed on the tumult of centuries and
the confusion of the individual soul. All men, *regardless of what historical,
geographical, ethnic, or ethical climate,* have found their most profound
enjoyment, which consists simply in the most intense "oblivion of the self,"
in rolling themselves up in the tenacious spirals of aesthetic oblivion. This
sublime oblivion can be recognized in the gesture of the shepherd, white or
black or yellow, sculpting the branch of a tree in the desolation of his
solitude. But in all the centuries before our own, among all the peoples of
the earth, the two Arts, with their four complements, remained identical.
What the international phalanxes of pedants thought they could call "the
evolution of the Arts" is simply a logomachy.

Our time is incomparable in inward and outward vigor in the creation of
the inner and outer world, in the production of hitherto unsuspected powers: internal and external, physical and religious.

And our time has synthesized with divine élan the multiple experiences
of man. And we have fully combined the life of practice and the life of
feeling, we have married Science and Art (I mean to say the discoveries and
not the postulates of Science and the ideals of Art) applying them together
to capture and to fix the rhythms of light—that's Cinema.[9]

In succeding essays, Canudo was critical of the contemporary
cinema. He argued that it was not the public but the film
businessmen who insisted on appealing to the lowest common de-
nominator:

I've seen the public of the most active and interesting working-class district of Paris, mechanics and factory-workers, hiss a crude melodrama that was supposed to be popular. Thus, they were demanding a cinema elevated above daily banality towards nobler states of the spirit. It's the characteristic of every art to satisfy this very general spiritual need, which consists in always tending from the beast to God. It's the characteristic of all art to renew the nations and their deepest life. Cinema can no longer be an exception.[10]

Canudo also argued that the attempt to imitate theater could lead nowhere, because there was nothing in common between theater and cinema.

Because of his high ambitions for the "Seventh Art," Canudo was particularly critical of the state of cinema. Cinema was a new language, and it was necessary to learn how to use it; it was also necessary to develop an aesthetic. Cinema was "an essentially universal language" with the capacity of "multiplying the human sense through expression by the image." It could stop the fleeting instant, conquer the ephemeral. By slow motion, it could depict vegetal birth, by use of simultaneous imagery, increase the sum of our sensations. Cinema could reveal nature as a person, make manifest the subconscious and the immaterial, areas which no art had been able to approach and which, Canudo believed, only music had been able to suggest. Canudo contended that the world was passing through its gravest crisis, a crisis even deeper than that of the collapse of the Roman Empire or of the Middle Ages after A.D. 1000. This essentially spiritual crisis could only be resolved by the creation of a vision common to all mankind, "Capable of satisfying the most profound aspirations of our souls, without offending our critical and analytical mentalities, which feel repugnance for all blind faith and for all disordered mysticism."[11] Music, the paradigm of universal harmony, would provide the cosmogony for a new mystical religion which could put man into direct contact with God.

In an earlier work entitled *The Musical Psychology of Civilization*, Canudo had argued that music would become the religion of the future: "Music is the supreme conceivable subtilization of earthly matter; it is similar to Light; like Light, it envelops Life."[12] Canudo was therefore interested in Elie Faure's assertion that cinema could produce "visible symphonies." Apparently he believed that the cinema, likewise a form of "music" which had the capacity to make visible the unseen and unconscious, would play an important role in what he termed the musical religion of the future.

The art historian Elie Faure was another significant aesthetician of the Seventh Art. Faure went further than Canudo in seeing cinema as the basis for a new religion. Faure (1873–1937) studied at the celebrated Lycée Henri IV under Bergson, by whom he was obviously influenced. He pursued medicine, but soon found his career as an art critic and historian. He wrote art criticism for *L'Aurore*, the newspaper of Clemenceau. It was *L'Aurore* which published Zola's famous *J'Accuse;* it is hardly surprising that Faure participated in the Dreyfus affair. Although Faure was politically involved only once again, as a supporter of the Republic during the Spanish Civil War, his republican sympathies were demonstrated by teaching at the popular university "La Fraternelle." His lectures there became the basis for his famous *History of Art*, which depicted art as the reflection of the life of civilization. In short, Faure was both an extreme idealist and a sound republican.

Elie Faure believed cinema would teach man a new language whose richness and complexity would not be exhausted by time. So impressed was he by the potential of the medium that he believed the invention of the cinema was equalled only by man's discovery of fire. Faure thought that the cinema could transform man on both an aesthetic and social level. It would provide a common spectacle for all mankind. As such, it could serve a vital role in the transformation of an individualistic, impulsive, and anarchic civilization into a new world of "plastic civilization" which would substitute "synthetic mass poems" for "analytic studies of states of mind and mental crises." Faure shared the disgust of many of his generation with the atomistic world of the nineteenth century, and like many of the Romantics, looked for a return to an organic society; unlike the Romantics, however, he did not preach a return to the Middle Ages, but the creation of a new form of social solidarity based on technology. It was not the machine that was to blame for man's spiritual crisis, but man's failure to use the machine. The cinema could reintegrate man into the very heart of the spiritual.[13]

Faure saw a parallel between the cinema and the medieval cathedral: "Film, like the temple," he stated, "is anonymous." Like the cathedral in the Middle Ages, cinema requires financial means greater than those of an individual, as well as the collaboration of a mass of craftsmen. Just as the cathedral emerged after a period of conflict from which an international Christian civilization crystallized, so film emerges alongside such collective phenomena as radio, syndicalism, economic trusts, and communism. If Catholicism formed the basis for revolutionary medieval society, the encyclopedia, socialism, and science provide the basis for today's. Faure declared that "those who place in opposition Christian faith and revolutionary passion see the latter from the outside. Thirst for the beyond is not exclusively the characteristic of mystics. All collective hope is a vehement aspiration to unity with God":

It would therefore be pointless to insist that faith is lacking here, to offer that faith which enabled architecture to spring from the soil of Western Europe in the twelfth century as a stepping-stone to a new mystical élan. In the presence of phenomena of this breadth, the old religions which offer themselves seem like worm-eaten planks, repainted several times, which people who don't know how to swim cling to when a ship sinks. Be calm. Cinema has just begun. The new faith shall find its aesthetic framework. . . . Faith is derived from the mysterious harmony between the intrinsic development of an art and the mystique which it is called upon to serve.

Faure goes on to explain the nature of this new mystique:

A sort of pantheist life must surge forth to the light from the interior unfolding of our spiritual universe. All its secret passages shall join our substance to the visible passages which the Cinema wrests ceaselessly from the world's inertia. This condition for new ecstasies had seemed hopeless since the death of all the gods. . . . For the first time, the infinite diversity of the world offers to man the *material* means to demonstrate its unity. With tireless willingness, a plea for universal communion offers itself to all. Its investigation demands nothing of us but a little good will. Let it not be denied. Let us not invoke the soul—always the soul!—in contrast to matter. The soul fastens its colossal vault only at the crossing of ribs which surge forth at one stroke from the depths of the earth. It is in the bread and the wine that the flesh and the blood and the spirit live.[14]

Faure believed that art should integrate man, society, and nature. He considered dance to be the primal art, which linked the individual "overly charged with consciousness" to the rhythm of the masses. The plastic arts, however, lacked the element of time. Film, by adding the dimension of time, would enable the plastic arts to provide a collective spectacle capable of bringing together an entire community and defining its moral order. This kind of collective art was the very antithesis of the theater, which to Faure epitomized the anarchic individualism of modern society. Faure denied that cinema and theater had anything in common, and decried the cinema's aping of theater.

Faure had a "painterly" view of cinema. He even imagined a cinema in which the actor *(cinémime)* would be replaced by visual symphonies even more moving than music. Faure held that plot was not fundamental to cinema. Plot merely established a skeletal framework for motion pictures. What really counted was the purely visual effect of cinema:

I distinctly remember how one day I came to understand what the future of the cinema could be. I was shocked to notice all of a sudden the magnificent relationship between a black garment and the grey wall of an inn. From that time on, I paid no more attention to the martyrdom of the poor woman, condemned to give herself to the lewd banker who had previously killed her mother and prostituted her child in order to save her husband from dishonor. With increasing wonderment I discovered that, thanks to the relationship of tones which transformed the film for me into a system of shades graduated from white to black and ceaselessly mixed, I was present at an unexpected animation. I descended into the crowds of individuals I had already seen, but only immobile, on the canvasses of El Greco, Rembrandt, Velasquez, Vermeer, Courbet, and Manet.[15]

A third important aesthetician of the Seventh Art was Jean Epstein, whom Abel Gance once called "a modern projection of Spinoza." Epstein was born in 1897, the son of a French father and a Polish mother, and came to France in 1908. He studied both engineering and medicine, demonstrating in his studies "a clarity and precision which were in stunning contrast with his sensibility and his magnetism."[16] But he was destined for other things. Soon he began to work for Auguste Lumière, one of the early experimenters in France who attempted to record imaginative "reality" on film. In 1920, together with his friends Lumière, Léger, the abstract artist, and Cendrars, the novelist, he founded *Le Promenoir*. In 1921 he became an assistant to the filmmaker and theoretician Louis Delluc. The next year, having published *La Lyrosophie* and directed *Pasteur*, Epstein had become a leading exponent of the avant-garde. Among his contributions as director were his experiments with the use of speeded-up motion in *La Glace à trois faces* and of slow motion in *The Fall of the House of Usher*. The latter film, made in 1928, is also remarkable in its creation of atmosphere, in its distortions of time, and in its conveyance of psychological tension. It is extraordinarily inventive in its use of camera movement and placement and in its special effects to create a supernatural ambience— the fracturing of images to suggest the fracturing of time, and its ghostly superimpositions. Another important experiment was

Epstein's use of unprofessional actors in *Finis Terrae* and *L'Or des Mers*. Epstein shared Canudo's aspirations for the cinema. Describing an ascent of Mt. Etna in a work entitled *Le Cinématographe vu de l'Etna*, Epstein writes:

> As we mounted to the crater on mule back, parallel to the flow of lava, I thought of you, Canudo, you who put so much soul into things. I believe you were the first to feel that cinema united all the kingdoms of nature into one, that of the greatest life. It puts the divine everywhere. Before me at Nancy a room of three-hundred persons groans aloud seeing a grain of wheat groaning on the screen. There suddenly appeared the true face of life and death, that of frightful love, which wrests such religious cries. What churches we should build, to shelter this spectacle in which life is revealed, if only we knew how to construct them.

Cinema would show all things in their divine and symbolic aspect. The lens of the camera was what Apollinaire would have characterized as the surreal eye, endowed with inhuman analytic qualities. It would show things in a way that we are no longer able to see them, free of our prejudice and morality. This analytic force differentiates cinema from theater.

Epstein believed the cinema revealed an essentially pantheistic world, a world permeated by the spirit expressed in multiple ways:

> I shall even say that the cinema is polytheist and theogenic. In bringing forth objects of the shadows to the light of interest, it creates beings that have scarcely any relationship to human life. These beings are parallel to amulets, greegrees, threatening objects and taboos of certain primitive religions. I believe that if one wants to understand how an animal, a plant, a rock can inspire respect, fear, horror, the three sacred feelings, they must be seen living on the screen—mysterious, mute, and strange to human sensibility.

Reality and poetry become one: "Here we enter the promised land, the country of the great wonder. . . . All nature, all objects appear as a man dreams them; the world is made as you believe it is. . . . Poetry is therefore true and exists as truly as the eye. The cinema is the most powerful means of poetry, the most real medium of the unreal, of the surreal, as Apollinaire would have said."[17]

For Canudo, Faure, and Epstein, cinema was not merely a Seventh Art. It was a means, rather, *the* means, of making manifest to man the real and mystical nature of existence. Nothing could be

more important, more revolutionary, than the development of this
new language. It was Abel Gance whom Epstein characterized as
"the present master of us all," who was recognized as the leader of
those determined to create this kind of cinema.

Gance had absorbed many of the main intellectual currents of his
time. From the day that he read *The Birth of Tragedy*, he became a
disciple of Nietzsche. He was especially impressed by Nietzsche's
energy and assertiveness, and, specifically, by Nietzsche's concept
of the tragic hero. Gance was also influenced by the Romantic interpretation of history, particularly by Hegel's notion of the World
Historical Individual, and by the Lamarckian theory of transformation (or evolution). Another major influence was the mystic tradition
of the sixteenth and seventeenth centuries, particularly the writings
of Jacob Boehme, and other occultists and theosophists. This is not,
however, an all-inclusive list. The ideas of Schopenhauer and
Bergson certainly had their impact. The point is that Abel Gance
was very widely read, and his intellectual tastes were omnivorous
and eclectic.

As an extreme idealist, Gance concerned himself with man's relationship to the Absolute rather than his relationship to society. For
Gance, the real epic was the cosmic drama and not the conflict of
individuals and society or of class against class. Gance draws many of
his ideas from pantheist and mystic thinkers, such as the seventeenth-century mystic Jacob Boehme. Discussing Boehme, the historian Alexandre Koyré argues that it is hardly coincidental that
those who pursue the regeneration of the spiritual life should be
attracted by vitalist conceptions of the universe. This is surely the
case with Abel Gance, who wanted to use his art as a weapon of
spiritual revolution. Gance returns to the anthropomorphic and
mystical universe which Boehme had known and which the scientific revolution had destroyed. In this universe, the divine is immanent; it flows through all things. There is no clear separation between man and god, or between animate and inanimate. All things
are alive, although they exist in varying degrees of perfection.

For Boehme, like the other Renaissance mystics, life and nature
were one: "all is living and the universe in its entirety is an eternal
river of life. The river spreads and breaks into separate and multiple
currents; the currents encounter each other, struggle, fight. Coming from one and the same source, they lose themselves in the same
ocean of life."[18] Nature is magical and magic natural. Man com-

prehends all; he is the microcosm of the universe. For Paracelsus, one of the chief representatives of the age, the human soul could affect the world soul. Our imaginings can influence the world soul which can in turn actualize them in the world. (One can readily understand why such a doctrine might be of particular interest to an artist who would want to impose his artistic vision on the world at large.) Paracelsus also believed that there is a process by which the material universe, expressing the astral, but only imperfectly, transfigures itself upward. The emblem of this process is alchemy. The alchemist in his laboratory simply tries to speed up this process. Is not the artist, then, a kind of alchemist, who attempts to bring men's souls closer to the divine?

Gance follows this way of thinking. Noting that the Greeks did not distinguish between animate and inanimate matter, he asserts that in Ionian philosophy all real existence came from ideas of a spiritual nature. Matter is only a confused reflection of the form. For Gance, all matter is pregnant with becoming:

The humblest matter tends to be or become something else. (Geology furnishes us proofs of this evolution.) To do so, it sometimes takes the external appearance of "life," for life, in short, is only an external appearance. Strictly speaking, there is no matter which is not living. Thus it is necessary to admit the existence and fact of the spiritualization of all that exists. From this I arrive at idealist spiritualism, which claims that mineral matter is not, in short, anything other than a sort of spirit of inferior quality whose evolution is too slow for us to distinguish any trace of life because of our false idea of time.[19]

Jean Epstein shares this notion. He writes that through the use of slow motion it is possible to depict the life of crystals, for example. Thus matter does not die, but constantly recreates itself.

These notions are roughly in line with the modern scientific refusal to draw a sharp line between living and dead matter. Recent experimentation has shown how amino acids, the very basis of life, can be built up under laboratory conditions. More and more it would seem that the development of life is related to an inherent tendency of chemicals to combine into increasingly complex configurations.

Thus far, Gance's ideas are consonant with much of what modern science is suggesting today. But Gance insists on picking up many old mystic notions and in formulating extravagant ideas based on a lack of full understanding of what science has shown. For example, Gance holds that matter is merely a form of electromagnetic energy, and science would agree with him that matter and energy are two faces of the same force. But Gance insists on seeing natural laws in anthropomorphic terms, or "sympathies," and it is there that his speculations become eccentric. Gravity thus becomes a case of Universal Love: "all beings struggle between the instincts of conservation and the desire to give themselves to that which is above them." Death, too, is a matter of appearances: "death is the rupture of the idea of time and space, but the fourth dimension persists and if you see with the third eye, you will see life anew across death." Gance quotes the eighteenth-century *philosophe* Robinet's assertion that all matter is composed of germs which develop when placed under favorable conditions: "the earth, the sun, the stars are enormous animals, whose size is too great for us to perceive their real nature."[20]

What Gance objected to most was the combination of a mechanistic view of the universe with the notion of the fixity of the species. This conception reduced the universe to a clock, uniform and repetitive in its motions and function. Gance seized upon Lamarck's conception of biological evolution, or transformism, as a means of seeing the universe as a living organism constantly striving towards a higher level of existence.

Gance considers Lamarck a poet, like Paracelsus—for he sees them both as connecting links between science and philosophy. Unlike the mathematicians, they were not confined by the notions of Time and Space. Gance believes Lamarck developed in a scientific fashion the concept of evolution intuited by Paracelsus. Gance constantly repeats the Lamarckian conception that "Desire creates the need, the need creates the function, the function creates the organ."

This, once again, was far from an idiosyncratic point of view. Most French scientists in the late nineteenth century preferred the Lamarckian to the Darwinian theory of evolution. This preference is perhaps understandable when we realize that whereas Darwin sees evolution largely as the result of accident, Lamarck sees it as a process of "unbroken progress." As the titular character of *Jean Barois* explains, from the initial monad: "Up to the most complicated manifestations of the human body and mind, there has been an unbroken progress lasting over hundreds of thousands of years.

And we owe it to this great thinker, Lamarck, that we now can trace and classify the various stages of that progress."[21]

Gance's admiration for Lamarck was shared by Elie Faure, who depicts him in much the same way Gance treats the tragic heroes of his films. According to Faure's biography, Lamarck "possessed the magnificent instinct of the predestined genius who knows he will live long enough to accomplish his task," an idea echoed in Gance's own later statements and an article of belief for the filmmaker in his advanced years.[22] Faure sees a similarity between Lamarck (who went blind) and Beethoven, (who went deaf), and Faure believes that these infirmities made possible their greatest insights. It is significant that this theme is central to Gance's *Beethoven*, and that Gance planned to make a film about Lamarck as part of his series of *Les Grands Initiés*. Both Gance and Faure derived an essentially Bergsonian concept of spiritual, creative evolution from Lamarck's theories of biological evolution.

Gance believes that imagination creates new needs and spiritual pleasures that produce the idea of the better, a wish to transcend the present state. This desire then becomes the basis for a new spiritual evolution of man. Gance also believes that such an evolution could be very rapid: "Butterflies take twenty minutes to pass from the state of larvae to the state of the butterfly. Possibility of an *extraordinary* rapidity if it is prepared for a great while." This hope of producing a great spiritual breakthrough is the goal of Gance's art. For this reason, Gance insists on making epics. The belief that a man's life lasts long enough for him to complete his mission, and that even after death one's soul continues to exert its influence, has sustained him in his struggle:

All which occurs, all which is produced in the brain has no need of being captured in the matrix of language or in the notes of the musician. By the very fact that something is conceived, it exists and cannot die. A powerful intuition alone can guide me because it is difficult to explain how the brain of a genius *who dies can radiate after him what he hasn't written*. Can't psychic waves round their circle after death without any support other than the projection of the will of the deceased in Time?

Even if the work of the artist is destroyed, before being beheld, it still maintains its occult power, invisible and mysterious:

The Time is ripe for a great spiritual Revolution: The Time is coming soon. The parables are worn. The dynasty is forming: new forces shall burst out at

our signal. The silence of my smile begins to frighten me myself. Time is
marching on and words, the Judases of our kingdom, shall soon be useless. . . . There is little to lose, and much to gain in this abandonment of our
poor daily maladroit egotism. Will you follow me if I am the first to open the
hands?

What is the nature of this evolution? Gance believes he has found
the secret of the universe in a kind of geometric mystery, Pytha-
goras' secret of the spiral:

In truth there is the triangle, the circle, the wheel, and the spiral. With its
invisible symbol the triangle dominated the millennia of Egyptian religion;
Christ stopped it; the cross is formed merely of four triangles whose bases
were just cut by a superior humanity. And then the cross began to turn, to
rotate in the spirits and hearts, and that was the circle, the Wheel. And
tomorrow, the tomorrow which is not at the end of my arm but at the end of
my will, the symbolic reign of the spiral will arrive. . . . The wheel slowly
gives way to the spiral.
The wheel reigned mechanically and philosophically over the world for
centuries. The higher mechanical and philosophical formula is the spiral,
the endless screw, the helix of the plane, which turns while each of the
points of its force advances.
The wheel turns only in two dimensions; the spiral turns in three.
This manner of seeing things which I conceived several years ago is for
me the most important of philosophical intuitions. All my life, all my work
turns not according to the Wheel, but according to the Spiral.[23]

Gance believed that modern society was far from utopian and that
real advancement must be moral and spiritual rather than material.
Man was still tied to the Wheel, unable to escape the burden of
history until the advent of a great spiritual revolution which would
enable man finally to make his own history. Gance is not alone in
wishing to use geometric symbolism to give sense to the meaning of
history. William Butler Yeats, in *A Vision*, develops similar ideas, as
does Canudo in his *Musical Psychology of Civilization*: "We are
accustomed to consider all evolution according to a spherical form,
or according to the unfolding of a spiral line. We know that all moves
away from the ancient but always returns there after a certain time,
without nevertheless repeating it in an absolute or definitive fashion. . . . The circular factum of the spiral line serves considerably to
enlighten our ideas about historical matters, and to explain the true
spirit of periods of 'return to the antique.' "[24]

Gance's work is the study of the conflict between Fatality and Destiny. The geometric symbolism contained in the passage just quoted from Gance's *Prisme* is the most important leitmotif in his films. Indeed, one might say that, visually speaking, it is far more powerful in expressing the conflict between the will to create a New Age and the forces which hold man down and destroy him. The symbol of the Wheel is the predominant image in three of Gance's most significant films: the first *J'Accuse*, *La Roue*, and *Beethoven*.

Who will be the agent of the great historical change, of the great spiritual revolution Gance foresees? Gance shares the Hegelian concept of history in claiming that it is the Great Man who is the agent of historical renovation. Indeed, for Gance there is no difference between the Great Man and the god: a god is merely one who is in advance of his time in the linear sense of evolution. Each spiritual renovation involves the birth of a new god; a greater one than the previous. This process of the creation of new gods is necessary because of the corruption of religions: "Gods create a dogma; the crowd believes in that dogma; the gods then become slaves of their teachings and cannot advance further."

Gance's writings and films, both those which were actualized and those which were only conceived, are about the great creators, the gods of human history.

The great creators are victimized by nature: Prometheus, Homer, Christ "are cruelly punished by nature for having stolen a secret." They are likewise punished by men "who also like to crucify their gods." Thus, "the most difficult thing for a genius is not to be a genius, but to live. . . ."[25] The fate of the great tragic heroes of Gance's films is hard: Hellé in the play *The Victory of Samothrace* sacrifices her life to gain immortality; Jean Diaz and Jean Novalic lose their minds for having brought an end to war. But in order truly to understand Abel Gance, one must recognize that he sees himself in a similar role. It is not by accident that Gance plays the part of Novalic in *La Fin du Monde*.

The identification of the World Historical Individual and the creator with gods, the deification of the hero, and the humanization of the divine is also an aspect of the influence of theosophy in Gance's thought. Theosophy is founded on the belief that all religions are based on a central truth which has been revealed in their esoteric doctrines. Theosophy also accepts the existence of occult powers, continuing the Renaissance belief in the essentially magical

quality of the universe. The goal of theosophy, in the words of
Madame Blavatsky, is "to reconcile all religions by showing the
identity of their origin, and to establish a universal belief based on
morality."[26] One of the most famous popularizations of this doctrine
is Edouard Schuré's *Les Grands Initiés, Esquisse de l'histoire se-
crète des religion,* first published in 1889 and going through over
one hundred editions in forty years. Denouncing what he considered to be the false idea of progress of the nineteenth century,
Schuré argues that the only true progress is spiritual. Schuré claims
that all the sages and prophets of all times have had the same beliefs
at heart, and attempts to prove this by a comparative study of their
esoteric doctrines. He discusses such people as Rama, Krishna,
Moses, Christ. Schuré classifies his position as one of intellectual
monism, evolutionary and transcendental spiritualism. His influence
on Gance is obvious.

Abel Gance certainly shares this basic point of view. Indeed, one
of his great dreams was to make a series of films entitled *Les Grands
Initiés,* which would set out to prove, through the study of all the
great religious leaders and poets, that all religions are really saying
the same thing. From this, it follows that Gance, despite his frequent use of Christian iconography, is not really operating from a
Christian perspective. He does not accept the exclusive truth of the
Christian cult. Christ was divine, but in the same sense that all of
the great *illuminés* of human history were divine. Moreover, the
Christian religion, like all religions, is an historical phenomenon.
New gods are being born; mankind's spiritual progress continues.

For Gance, the goal of art is the same as spiritual creation. But
what exactly is artistic creation and by what means can art bring
about the great changes which Gance desired? According to Gance,
the artistic experience occurs "when someone dictates and I write,
despite myself. There is a mysterious explosion of the subconscious
which I cannot control and which is capable one day of projecting
my reason to the stars. . . ." Gance wonders whether it isn't a
"subconscious reflex of the Will to hide *what one knows,* what for
thousands of years we have not wanted to recognize." It is not
thought, but the intuitive conception "by which all real works of art,
all immortal ideas, have received the spark of life."[27] Indeed, Gance
claims that intuition is the memory of the future. There are two
kinds of artists, those who record what is, and those who create new
forces directly.

Gance, feeling himself charged with an enormous mission, has always fluctuated between the sense of being able to bring about world-shaking changes and a sense that the time was not ripe, or that his powers were insufficient. In an interview in *Filma* in 1920, Gance explained that he could have done much more in cinema, but that it was first necessary to teach the visual alphabet to the people, since cinema is essentially a social and international art.[28] Nevertheless, even in the 1920s Gance experienced a sense of frustration, a sense of personal regression at being obliged to put off his great works. How much greater the frustration he felt after the retirement of Charles Pathé, who had supported Gance financially, and who had given him a free hand artistically. Since the end of the 1920s, how many of his projects have lain untouched in his desk, how many scenarios have been buried at the bottom of the great piles of manuscripts which fill his apartment? Gance noted that the lack of success tended to bring out "a certain epicurean indolence," perhaps a certain fatalism. Just like his characters, Gance feels himself to be the battleground of the forces of Destiny and Fatality. And, sadly. Gance's old age resembles that of the artists and creators depicted in his films.

Prisme, which the filmmaker published in 1930, traces Abel Gance's search for an art form which would enable him to express the plentitude of his ideas, which would enable him to bring about, perhaps, that metamorphosis of caterpillar man into human butterfly. In the "Avertissement" of *Prisme,* Gance admits that he did not have "the courage to prepare to the very end this mute explosion capable of projecting men 'into the ecstasy of gold and emeralds' " which he wished for them.

But for the young Gance, the choice of an art form was difficult. Gance began his career as an actor, and soon became a playwright. But Gance sought a new form. Certain of his mission, he was uncertain of his path. A new form of art had to be created to lift men from the contemplation of lower things, to help them find the real path of joy, to open the locks of desire: "To floor the accelerator of the imagination, to create new intellectual ambiences favorable to the blossoming of new senses, *to create a reality the cube of that which we now live.*"

A new language was necessary. Around 1910 Gance writes:

How? Where? Alliterations? Philosophies? Onomatapoeias? What doors must be opened before the unseizable which we feel in us and which smiles at all our verbiage, even the highest. Our words, passing by our senses, become deformed and take a poetical value of embellishment which kills their essential value. It is not a question of an original way of expressing what we know but of the discovery of a new instrument which would be more subtle, more pointed, more ethereal, more divine, with which we could finally open the locks of the unknown, the unconscious kingdoms within, accessible with difficulty to our senses and totally inaccessible to our words. . . . What I seek has not yet been thought. It is the language of silence.

What we call music is generally only organized noises. What I call silence is the eternal and colossal vibration of all the music of the world, like light is the vibration of all the colors of the prism.

Do I make myself better understood in saying this?

Music is silence which awakes.

Silence is light which slumbers.

Gance believes that this silence lies in the electromagnetic spectrum between audible sounds and visible light and speculates that the gods have used these vibrations to communicate with mankind, directly, and without words:

Will I be understood if I express my regret that Christ was obliged to speak? The gods of Mahomet, Buddha, Moses, Brahma did not speak directly as far as I know. They probably employed this invisible form of vibration, more powerful than electricity, to communicate to their prophets in order to translate their dogmas into popular language. . . . The soul can speak without words just as the telegraph communicates without the wire. Trees have always spoken to the fountains, light speaks to the birds, the ocean speaks to the sky, our soul speaks to us, and deaf, blind, and proud, we don't listen and we understand nothing. Let us attempt to hear these silent conversations. Who wants to help me put a microphone on the real heart of the world?

Gance speculates on what new means to use:

Doubtless some strange matter will enter into it, a sort of plate sensitive to the states of the soul, perhaps a photograph of the sensibility. . . . Physiological excitation of the spirit, whence a conversion of all into images, trances, to materialize within. X-Ray, cinema, I don't know, but I shall have to pass long hours developing all this lyrically, intuitively, scientifically.

Gance's interest in cinema was related to the theology of light. Gance was influenced by Pseudo-Dionysius the Areopagite (who

had already influenced Abbot Suger, the creator of the first Gothic
cathedral). Gance believed, like Suger, and Boehme, that light was
a bridge between the noumenal and phenomenal world; the second
stage of the art of the future would be symphonies of light:

I must surrender myself to the artistic study of colored vibrations. It is the
music of the future. Until infra-red/ultra-violet vibrations are discovered for
us. But with what money, my god, shall I make this clavier on which to play
light?

Gance originally saw cinema merely as a means of making money.
He thought of himself as a writer. At about the same time, René
Chomette began to employ the pseudonym René Clair for films, so
that he could use his real name for "serious" literature. Eventually,
however, around the time of *Mater Dolorosa* and the *Tenth Symphony*, Gance recognized the enormous potential of cinema. It is
then that a great event, almost a miracle, took place in the cinema.
Abel Gance made *J'Accuse,* a film which breaks out of the entire
genre of melodrama.

On July 16, 1922, Abel Gance and Blaise Cendrars pondered the
question of the new art form. Gance said that if a new god were to
surge forth, and looked at the world, he would exclaim: "If all my
predecessors have failed despite their magnificent souls and the
inestimable treasures that they left the earth, if the only result
they've achieved with man is that he walks bent like cattle under the
yoke of money, I'm afraid of recommencing the same story. Blood
will be spilled unnecessarily for my doctrine to triumph over the
others. Let's see about some other stars. . . ."[29]

Gance as a mystic believed in the unity of the world, and in the
need for direct contact between man and the divine immanent in all
things. Film, an electronic rather than a mechanical medium, to use
McLuhan's terminology, seemed able to provide that instantaneity
and unity. This was indeed the Promised Land, where all thoughts
and dreams became true, where montage and cutting could bring
together what normally seemed most disparate, where the Third
Eye of synthesis could break through old habitudes of perception, of
the old sensibility. Is it surprising that Gance meditated so long on
the nature of electronic waves? Is it surprising that Gance is one of
the few today to sense the future of an art based on the holograph?
Intuitively and *before* the fact, he sensed what McLuhan came to
tell us *after* the fact.

Gance was therefore a founder of the Seventh Art, both as a theorist and as a practitioner, not despite his world view but because of it. The artistic sensibility, seeking an end to a social and artistic world based on analysis and atomism, discovered a medium which provided the basis for an entirely new, modern sensibility. It was the Marriage of Feeling and the Machine, as Canudo had predicted.

J'Accuse footage arranged in Polyvision triptych for *Magirama*.

3

Gance's Accusations Against War: *J'Accuse* (1919), *La Fin du Monde* (1929), *J'Accuse* (1938)

WITH THE CREATION OF *J'Accuse* (completed and released in 1919), a new epoch begins in the career of Abel Gance and in the history of the French cinema. It is nearly impossible to convey the extraordinary experience one undergoes in seeing the original *J'Accuse;* one comes away from it with the impression that Gance himself must have gone through the same kind of rapid evolution which he prophesied for mankind. *J'Accuse* is a complete and perfect work of cinema. It is not merely the precursor of a new art form: it is both precursor and perfect actualization. Gance, and the French cinema with him, has come into his own.

The achievement of *J'Accuse* arises from and depends upon Gance's reaction to political events in Europe, linked to a profound sense of personal frustration and an existential need for self-expression. In a notebook entry of June 14, 1917, Gance appears to be spiritually defeated, adrift and lacking purpose in the swirl of circumstances surrounding him: "The new year hardly differs from the old," he writes, "presenting the same crepuscular joys and the same lacunae. I live on the border of the war, a seaweed thrust onto the strand. I am farther from myself than ever. I no longer find myself, so to speak. All my thoughts, my very work, are lost in a fog. I live perpetually exhausted with only the idea of doing well what I am doing at the moment, and that's all."

By the following year, however, the filmmaker had clearly recovered his sense of mission and purpose. In a notation written in 1918 and recorded in *Prisme*, Gance recalls his state of mind as he embarked upon the production of *J'Accuse:*

I begin *Ecce Homo*, a sort of vast prologue to the gigantic fresco of *Royaume de la Terre* and *La Fin du Monde*, but I quickly perceive that my subject is too elevated for everything around me, even for my actors, who don't exude a sufficient radioactivity. I will kill myself very quickly if I continue to

ndreds of soldiers spell out the title J'Accuse *(1919) in
nce's first "accusation against war."*

generate this high voltage to no purpose. I stop the film one-third finished, and I return to my films concerning the war and its lesson, because they are much closer to the mentality of the spectators.

I execute my film *J'Accuse*. I am penetrated with an invincible confidence in my cinematographic power, tempered by the blindness of the public. . . . And by my health, which leaves me prostrate for entire weeks.

I have just finished the exteriors of *J'Accuse*. Time and circumstances have been favorable. I consider this work with confidence. I believe that the social significance of *J'Accuse* is profound and that the film will triumph everywhere and nothing will shackle its purpose. The "dead who return" sequence must give the results that I was seeking: to make the gulls who remain humans think.[1]

J'Accuse marks the emergence of a distinctive style that is poetically evocative, rhythmically evolving, and deeply psychological. In this film Gance has attained that capacity to express himself through the rhythmic utilization of the visual which characterizes his later work; the cadences of the visual images are as real as those of a symphony. Montage and superimposition effectively enter the world of French film; and though the camera may still be stationary (with the exception of some remarkable travelling shots), the viewer experiences no ennui. The use of heightened contrasts and fine composition, already evident in *Mater Dolorosa,* is now general. Tinting makes it possible to explore further the relationship of tone to psychological nuance. The red tints of the dead in battle scenes, the blues of rippling waters used to illustrate Jean Diaz's poetry—these marvelous tintings make us question whether "color" film necessarily marked an advancement with the development of the Technicolor process rather than a restriction of what could effectively be done with color.

This film speaks in visual terms: it has few titles; it doesn't need them. Moreover, in the person of Séverin-Mars, Gance has found an extraordinary *cinémime.* This actor, coming from the Comédie Française, brings none of the atavisms of the theater with him: as Jean Diaz (and later as Sisif in *La Roue*), Séverin-Mars can express all that is needed with the smallest gesture or expression. The quality of the acting contrasts favorably with Griffith's work. Perhaps that is one reason why *J'Accuse* does not appear to b ᵛ dated: it exists in its own universe of color, contrasts, and rhythms. If Abel Gance never did another film, this one alone would have earned him immortality. A perfect instrument had been created. Now it was possible to change the world.

J'Accuse is one of the first and perhaps the most moving film ever made about the horrors of war. It shows how war destroys the human community, but it also evokes the hope that an end can be made to war. The film places the interrelationships of a human community within a greater and metaphysical context.

The film begins with the scene of a *farandole* in the village. Gance creates an eerie effect by showing the faces of the dancers colored by the fire. This round dance is the first manifestation of what will become a major leitmotif in Gance's work: the wheel, representing fatality and the eternal return. We become acquainted with the dramatis personae of the film: the animalistic François Laurin, whose face and that of a dog are superimposed in the introduction, the François Laurin whom we see seated at a table with his hunting dog, the carcass of a fawn lying on the table, its blood dripping down and forming a puddle at Laurin's feet. Edith, his wife, is repulsed by his brutality and can find little understanding in her father, Maria Lazare, a veteran of 1870 who lives only for revenge. Edith finds consolation in Jean Diaz, a young poet who lives with his mother and who has written a sequence of poems called *Les Pacifiques*. At night, Jean recites these poems to his mother. As he reads the "Ode au Soleil," we see drawings of pastoral scenes, a sunrise over the water beautifully tinted. François Laurin is highly jealous of Jean. One day while hunting, he finds Jean and his wife together in the woods. In a stroke of dramatic genius, Gance has Laurin take out his gun and shoot . . . a bird.

The declaration of war brings scenes of almost orgiastic rejoicing. Skeletons dance the round; the Grim Reaper's scythe is superimposed with pages of the *Pacifiques*. Then poignant departures to war are shown, only by hands. We see hands clasping, praying; we see them taking a last glass of wine. François Laurin leaves, but he is afraid that Jean will take advantage of the situation in the month which remains to him before joining his regiment. He therefore sends his wife to visit his father in the Ardennes.

We see Maria Lazare together with the old men of the village, all dressed in old uniforms and medals, charting the course of the war on a map with pins. Maria receives a telegram announcing that his daughter has been deported by the Germans, who captured the town in which she was staying. Jean promises to avenge her. He abandons his pacifism. Imagining the deportees, Jean utters for the first time the phrase *J'Accuse* ("I accuse")!

Jean is sent as an officer to François's regiment, where he

encounters the latter's hatred. When the captain gives Jean orders for Laurin to undertake what will probably be a suicidal mission, Jean goes in his place. When he returns alive, they begin to communicate. They recognize that each loves Edith equally in his own way, and they share her memory together.

Weakened and ill, Jean returns home to care for his ailing mother. In an effective travelling shot we see him facing the beautiful natural setting of his town perched on a hill. He returns to the house. His mother asks him to recite the "Ode to the Sun." As he does so, we once again see the frames used to illustrate *Les Pacifiques*. When Diaz looks up, his mother is dead. She died at precisely the place where in the previous scene she had fallen asleep. He finishes the poem; the candles go out. Diaz now accuses a war which kills mothers as well as children.

Edith returns to the village—with a little girl. She had been raped by German soldiers in the Ardennes, and this violation leads to yet another accusation. Angèle, however, is innocence personified. She does not understand the meaning of death when she sees Jean's mother.

When François returns, he is suspicious of the story invented to explain the child's presence. One day, he tells his wife that the little child was drowned in the pond. In a remarkable sequence, we see Edith running, followed by shots of the pond, Edith running past a house, then barnyard animals running. But nothing has happened. She finds Jean there, playing with the child. François, believing that Jean is the child's father, grabs him by the throat. When Edith tells the true story, he is barely restrained from killing Angèle. It is clear to him that he must leave; but he cannot accept the thought of leaving Jean behind in the village with his wife. There is only one solution: both Jean and François return to the front.

Jean suffers from fever, and is carried away by poetic visions. The men listen to him preach the gospel of accusation; he is like a Christ of the trenches. Finally, before a crucial battle, Jean goes mad; in the battle, meanwhile, François receives a fatal wound. Lying on a bed next to Jean's, the dying François grasps Jean's hand, then dies (an idea that is reworked in the later version of the film. The 1938 sound version of *J'Accuse*, however, is considerably different from the silent motion picture of the same title in both plot and characterization, as will be seen; it is not simply a remake with sound added.) Rapid scenes of the battle are then followed by a slow travelling shot of the ruined choir of a church with bodies inside.

Preparation for the following scene is annotated in this passage from Gance's notebooks of November 1918 (recorded in *Prisme,* pp. 158–59):

The cemeteries refuse corpses every evening. First Act: Ruins. Second Act: Ruins. Last Act: Ruins. . . . How all unhappiness is alike. . . . And how I wish that all the dead of the war would rise up one night and return to their country, into their houses, to discover whether their sacrifices served for aught. War would stop on its own, strangled by the immensity of the horror. Until 1914 I had only suffered for myself. For two years, I have suffered for others, and have forgotten my own despair. I didn't know it could be so terrible . . . and I have only my body and my imprisoned and useless ideas. . . . All ideas are in concentration camps.

. . . To speak to them . . . to cry to them . . . to sing to them. . . . What voice can be heard in this typhoon? . . . my arteries spurt the sap of indignation and my veins bring back pity to my heart. To walk nude between two trenches, to make each side hesitate for fear of killing one of their own . . . because what one kills in war is not men, but uniforms, and because God is silent, both from the sky and from Rome . . . to create for several instants a Truce of Man each night when I pass, a spectre of the trenches. . . .

These ideas were fomenting in Gance's imagination and were to shape the next development in *J'Accuse.*

Jean escapes from the hospital and returns to the village, disheveled. He distributes a note to the inhabitants telling them to come to Edith's house that night for news of their dead. The light of the fireplace, suggested by orange tinting, colors the assembly as Diaz tells them: "—I was in a field at night as a sentry. A dead man was next to me. Suddenly, he rose and cried: 'My friends, my friends. . . . Let's go and see if the country is worthy of us and if our deaths have served some purpose.' I saw them surge forth, all the dead of the war. Anxiously, they helped each other and began to march towards the village. I began to run in front of the innumerable herd, and I am here to warn you. They are coming! And they will return to sleep with joy if their sacrifice and their death have done some good."

This scene of the dead arising is one of the most magnificent scenes in cinema. Diaz, with prophetic madness, accuses those few who were not worthy of their men. The guilty try to run away. The dead arrive, and they are happy to know that they did not die vainly. Diaz tells them to let the dead return. They want the people to remain courageous. The townspeople leave, consoled.

Jean Diaz is left alone with Edith. The experience was too much for him: he has lost his sanity. Later, little Angèle guides Jean's hand in writing the words "J'Accuse," which he had once taught her.

The next day, Jean enters the room. He opens *Les Pacifiques*, laughs, and tears up the pages: the soldier in him has killed the poet. But then he comes to the "Ode to the Sun." He seems to recover his presence of mind. As sunbeams stream through the window, Diaz recites his poem to the sun. He accuses the sun of having witnessed the whole horrible epic of war. At this point, he falls down, dead. The sun streams over his body; then the sun sets, and the light ends. One recalls here what Gance has written in *Prisme* (p. 73): "One must leave the self through the gate of the eyes and be strong enough to repel the light of the day by the light of the soul. At that time, beware of the light of the day; it becomes jealous. Homer, Oedipus, Ossian, Milton, Handel, Galileo . . . because the light lives, I feel it, and the blind know it well. Especially beware of it when you transcend it." Diaz dies because he has transcended his ordinary human role.

Jean Diaz is the first of Gance's great tragic heroes in film, men who die or lose their minds by attempting to go beyond the limits of the human condition. The powers of Diaz the prophet are too great for Diaz the man: he is no longer able to function on a human level after seeing the light. For Diaz's sacrifice has brought back the dead to the audience of 1919. Certainly, Gance hoped that by this recording he could keep alive the memory of their sacrifices. The passionate performance of Séverin-Mars was only a performance; but many of the veterans who played the dead, the *gueules cassées*, the wounded of the war, did in fact die in the days following the filming. They in life, as Diaz in imagination, were giving their lives to prevent future war.

The political implications of this film are ambiguous. This is not surprising for a film made during the war. Gance shares the ambiguity of Diaz, who is opposed to the brutality of war itself, but who specifically accuses those he deems responsible for starting the war in the first place. Gance himself states that his purpose is "to show the horror of war and consecrate to the execration of the ages those who are responsible" (*Prisme*, p. 164). Gance explains that he had been inspired by Wilson's message to the American Senate which confirmed his ideas. The film thus combines pacificism, Wilsonian idealism, and a certain amount of French nationalism. Deeming that the Germans were responsible for the war and its atrocities, Gance had planned a scene in which Jean Diaz would recount in the hospital a vision of an Assize Court of the Peoples, in which a jury of neutrals and a Chief Justice resembling Christ would try those responsible. Another idea which was not cut is Diaz's story of the giant Gaul who incites the soldiers to victory. The interpretation of war guilt shifts considerably in the second version of *J'Accuse*.

Gance planned to follow *J'Accuse* with *Les Cicatrices* (The Scars) and *La Société des Nations* (The League of Nations); but these films were never made. He also planned *Ecce Homo*, *Le Royaume de la Terre*, and *La Fin du Monde*. This last film he was eventually able to complete, not immediately after *J'Accuse*, but some ten years later. The film is a successor to *J'Accuse*, however, and its hero, Novalic, is the spiritual brother of Jean Diaz.

La Fin du Monde is part of Abel Gance's attempt to resolve the problems of human society and in particular to eliminate war. The idea and title for the film are derived from a rather quaint and tedious novel by the astronomer Camille Flammarion, a work whose ostensible literary form barely hides a pedagogical goal. The work lacks any real characters and is, as the author himself suggests, didactic: in it, a comet is used as a "pretext for all possible discussions on this great and important subject—*The End of the World*." The near destruction of the earth by a comet comes in the twenty-fifth century, long after war has been eliminated, and after the international anarchist revolution of 1950, provoked by unbearably high taxes, has been followed by the resolution of the social issue.

Typically, Gance takes this raw material and transforms it almost completely, according to his own imagination. Excepting descriptions of the effects of the comet on the earth, there is nothing in common between the film and the novel on which it is based. We shall follow the description of Gance's *La Fin du Monde* in the Joachim Renez scenario, which presents the film as it was meant to be and not as it finally emerged through the stupidity of its producer, who took final control away from Gance.

In the *Fin du Monde*, war is averted by an outside force—the threat of the comet—and this, in turn, leads to the creation of the Universal Republic. In order to bring about change, an external force is needed. The central figure, Novalic, quotes Kropotkin in this regard: "There are times in the life of humanity when the necessity for a powerful shock, for a cataclysm to come and shake society to its very depths, imposes itself in all respects."

Men are not capable of reforming themselves. They do not listen to their prophets. Both Jean Novalic and Jean Diaz in *J'Accuse* bear the same message: "Love one another." But it is only because of their superhuman qualities and the complicity of superhuman forces that they finally succeed in propagating that message.

La Fin du Monde and the two versions of *J'Accuse* all revolve around the same typology: the major difference is that whereas there is only one hero in *J'Accuse,* a man who both thinks and acts, and who pays the price by sacrificing either his life or his sanity, in *Fin du Monde* there are two heroes. Jean Diaz has in effect been recreated as two brothers: the prophet Jean Novalic, the idealist author of the *Royaume de la Terre,* and his scientist brother, the astronomer, Martial Novalic, who executes his brother's plan. Like Gance, Novalic is a great synthesizer of ideas. We see on his desk at one time or another: the Bible, the Koran, the Talmud, the Vedas, the writings of Plato, Nietzsche, Spinoza, Marx, Lenin, Washington, Lincoln.

Novalic seems outside of his century. When Jean reads his brother the passage from Kropotkin, telling him that the time is now come, his brother replies, "Poet, you waste your time in investigating the thought of all these philosophies. These are theories and nothing more. You are poetry, love, the heart . . . but the modern world has taken its precautions against the sublime. *They cannot understand you;* you speak a language dead for your time."

But Jean's eyes convince Martial, despite himself. Jean Novalic provides the message of salvation, but must sacrifice earthly happiness and his love for Geneviève. His brother executes Jean's plan to save the world and finally wins Geneviève, whom he also loves. A victim of temporary madness, Jean disappears from an asylum before the catastrophe. He roams the streets, relating to people and things by seeing their reflections in a mirror he carries. After the renovation, his mirror is broken; he recovers lucidity and comes face to face with reality. Martial has married Geneviève; Jean Novalic has become the patron saint of the new religion. Jean makes one final renunciation: now that his work has been accomplished, his own personal existence is nothing but an obstacle. As the film ends, he disappears into the anonymous crowd. Such is the fate of gods, misunderstood in their time, forced to sacrifice themselves, and either killed by the people they try to help or forced into madness. Jean had already written in his book, *Le Royaume de la Terre:*

Men have pity for men, but they always crucify their gods. . . . If tomorrow the ideal incarnate returned to earth, he would still find himself in the face of wickedness that has to be tamed and of stupidity that has to be scoffed at.

Gance is also demonstrating his views of religion in this film. Religion is necessary, for how else can the transformation of man take place? Gance presents a mean and nasty world. Ambition, corruption, immorality, and lust are the dominant features—who reads the gospel which Jean Novalic peddles from a handcart?

The scenario is heavily archetypical and symbolic. At the beginning of the film, Jean Novalic (played, significantly, by Gance himself), is representing Christ in a passion play. So intense is his passion that he faints after the crucifixion. The apparently Christian construct of the *imitatio Christi* is doubtless something of a concession to European sensibilities. For Gance, all religions are branches of the same tree, and Christ is only one of many gods who have emerged to lead man in his spiritual evolution. Novalic is as much a god as Christ, Geneviève in her own right is a Mary Magdalene, and Schomburg, the plutocrat who sits in the audience, is the very incarnation of evil in the world. The essential plot in the scenario revolves around the conflict of Novalic and Schomburg over the fate of the world and that of Geneviève's soul.

Jean Novalic reminds us of Alyosha in the *Brothers Karamazov.* Indeed, the physical cause of his madness is being hit on the head with a stone thrown by someone in a crowd when he attempts to rescue a young girl who is being beaten up by her mother. Like Alyosha, Novalic feels an obligation to the poor: he lodges them in his house, only to be robbed by the very people he has helped. Luis Buñuel, of course, has also worked variations on this general pattern, in *Nazarín* and *Viridiana.*

If Novalic stands for a kind of god-figure, he is also the emblem of the cinematographer. Knowing that he is destined to go mad, knowing even before he is told by his brother that the earth is facing destruction—from which only the strong, courageous, and virtuous will come out alive—Novalic prepares a testament in records and films. Even while he is dead to the world, his message will save it.

This orgy scene from *La Fin du Monde* represents the moral chaos of a world in danger of colliding with a comet, an idea Gance obtained from the astronomer Camille Flammarion.

Thus Gance affirms his belief in cinema as a means of REVELA-TION which can hold its power even after the death of its creator.

For Martial Novalic to carry forth Jean's message, the only way mankind can be saved, he must be an opportunist. The new order of things must be prepared for before the cataclysm. To defeat Schomburg, the devil himself, Novalic must get the support of another banker, Werster, whose proclivities for young boys have already been evidenced. Werster supports Martial Novalic to defeat Schomberg, but is not destined to pass into the New World: "I played like a non-believer, and the truth kills me." Is this not also a statement of Gance's attitude toward film businessmen? Alas, this time it was the *cinéaste* and not the capitalist who failed. What the public eventually saw had little in common with Abel Gance's intentions.

The end of the film is a depiction of the Apocalypse. Mankind divides into two groups, those who engage in mad orgies as the end of the world approaches and who are condemned to death, and those who follow Jean Novalic's message. In the very last moments before the head-on crash with the comet is supposed to take place, Martial Novalic reads a constitution of the Universal Republic before a mass of cheering delegates. The destruction of one universe and the creation of another intersect. A new world is literally born out of the death of the old one. As Jean Novalic had said (mixing Christ and Nietzsche):

. . . In the last days preceding the end of the world all those who shall resist the terror will be forged forever for a future humanity. There is only one chance to escape the disaster. Only those shall escape who shall have replaced fear in their hearts by love. Humanity must cast aside those who are not born for victory. Only the strong shall remain.

Just before he loses himself in the crowd, Jean sees himself on a vast screen, saying:

I assure you in truth, the kingdom of the earth is composed of a single heart, a single love, a single country. I don't speak to you in the name of religion, but in the name of love. Make a religion of your love for men. I beg you on my knees.—Love the plant, the bird, the wind, the water, and even the stones. Love! Love! Love!

Nothing better demonstrates the irrationality of a social system which allows final decision-making concerning a work of art to be in the hands of a businessman than the terrible fate of *La Fin du Monde*. Not only did the failure of this film make it difficult for Gance to obtain the financing credits he needed to make further films; what is most tragic is that the film, one of Gance's major undertakings and probably a major work, was altered and thereby distorted beyond recognition.

Everything is truncated, the visual and sound sequences, the plot itself. Instead of the careful rhythmic sequences of images characteristic of Gance, we find primitive and jerky cutting from one scene to another. Gance has said in an interview that the producer of the film did the editing together with his janitor! Many of the scenes would be virtually unintelligible if one had not read the scenario. Instead of a philosophic statement about man and divinity, we have a kind of science-fiction story which retains enough discordant notes not to be convincing. Significant characters are never developed.

The identification of Novalic with God and of Schomburg with the Devil are lost, as is the sense of Novalic's message. Gance's condemnation of war disappears. (So does the scene in which Gance shows two people in a waiting room, one reading *L'Humanité* and the other *L'Action Française,* glaring at one another with hatred.) These ideas disappear, since the finished film virtually eliminates the notion that only a catastrophe could prevent war. The attack on ideological factionalism is thus deleted, as is Gance's identification of plutocracy with moral decay and war-mongering. Schomburg's lewdness and Werster's perverse fondness for young boys are cut. The epilogue barely remains. Novalic disappears from the film once he disappears from the asylum. The meaning of his life and sacrifice are therefore erased.

La Fin du Monde could have been a great film. Instead, it is a debacle. Its failure can only be measured in terms of its enormous potential. Its images cry for completion, its sounds for a proper chance to speak. What we see arouses as much anger as sorrow.

In 1938, Abel Gance directed a sound version of *J'Accuse.* This film is almost entirely different from the silent version. The main difference comes from the different situations at the times the two films were made. The first *J'Accuse* was intended to guarantee that the dead of the First World War had not died in vain. The second *J'Accuse,* written at a time when events were moving toward a new conflagration, was meant as an attempt at preventing the war. The first film starts before the outbreak of World War I and concludes in 1918; the second film begins with World War I and continues on until the 1930s. The Jean Diaz of 1938 is a different character: unlike his namesake of 1919, he is both dreamer and man of action—he is both Jean and Martial Novalic. But the romantic plot has been largely eliminated, and the film is more sober and straightforward.

The second *J'Accuse* owes much to *La Fin du Monde.* Whereas in *La Fin du Monde* it is the threat of a comet which unleashes the process by which the Universal Republic is proclaimed, in *J'Accuse* it is the threat of war and the returning of the dead which brings about a similar process with a similar outcome.

The later film is more than a social statement: it is cosmic drama. For Gance, war cannot be stopped by man alone, but only by the evocation of superhuman forces, the collective wisdom of man's experiences made immanent. Man can only be stopped from going to war by calling upon the dead of past wars to stop him. In attempting to place a social question within a universal framework, a framework demanded by his own religious and moral perspective, Gance the artist places an enormous burden upon his art. Such a film can either be ludicrous or overwhelming. The issue could have been humanized by means of a romantic plot, as in Ernst Lubitsch's *Broken Lullaby* or in Gance's own earlier version of this film. But his mature vision here is far more rigorous and uncompromising. For Abel Gance, it is not a question of melodrama, but of metaphysics. His hero, Jean Diaz, is totally dedicated to the memory of his fellow soldiers of the "Death Patrol." He alone of twelve men survives the last mission of the war. Carried back from the field with the others, wrapped in a shroud, his moans at the funeral allow him to be brought back, to arise from the dead, as if to become their emissary on earth. He had sworn to them that there would be no more war. He is never seen as father or lover; he is a man possessed by a mission.

The film begins at Douamont, a town in the center of the fighting. Its fountain is polluted with blood; a bleeding dove lies within; a crucifix hangs upside down. The world's order has been over-thrown. The film ends with Jean Diaz being burned at that very spot, now a monument to the dead of the war topped by the Virgin and Child. He is burned by his countrymen, whom he has frightened by raising the Army of the Dead. Jean Diaz, an inventor who had hoped to make war impossible by his inventions, is faced with the lot common to Gance's great men. They are turned against by those who do not understand them, who want to "crush their ideas and obliterate what they have done." For Gance, the great man is one who can make things the way he imagines them. He can appeal to forces within and without him which are superhuman. In *Napoléon*, Bonaparte is entrusted with the fate of the Revolution by the spirits of Danton, Robespierre, and Saint-Just. In the second *J'Accuse*, Diaz represents the dead and must ultimately call upon their aid to stop war. The world of the *noumena* is not just a met-aphor for Abel Gance. Jean Diaz is simultaneously a Neitzschean superman, a Christ-figure who dies for those he wants to save, and a personification of the director himself. For had not Gance made this new version of the film in an effort to stay the seemingly ineluctable march toward war? As stated before, the original version of the film was supposed to be the first part of a triptych that would include *The Scars* and *The League of Nations*. It was made in the hope that the

Great War would be the last. The sound version was made when
Gance began to despair of the international situation.

After the shots of the symbolic fountain and town at the beginning
of the film, the viewer is transported into "The Elephant Cabaret," a
café for soldiers. The songs heard there about "A Woman" are in-
terspersed with shots and sounds of cannon's firing. Flo, the singer,
shows an obvious interest in a young soldier, Gilles Tenant. Here,
we surmise, are the makings of a melodrama. What could be more
banal than a sentimental story about a singer and a soldier caught up
in World War I? The film, however, belies these expectations. Tenant is soon dead, and Flo, like Diaz, will devote her entire life to the
memory of the dead.

A reconnaissance patrol must be sent out that day. Of the previous "Death Patrol," only Diaz had returned alive. In the uncut
version, the order to carry out this useless patrol comes from Captain Henri Chimay of the General Staff, who overrules the company
commander. (This scene is cut from the Museum of Modern Art
print. Its existence is revealed by Roger Icart's book, *Abel Gance*.)
After the drawing of lots, Jean Diaz decides to take the place of one
of its twelve members, who is the father of four children. Diaz first
sacrifices himself for one individual, as later he will sacrifice himself
for all men.

The patrol's departure is soon followed by the death scene of
Gilles Tenant. Gilles, sinking progressively into a bog, calls desperately and vainly for help. Then his face changes expression. His
imaginings are visualized as we see a trumpeter calling the cease-
fire and are reminded of an earlier remark about how wonderful it
would be to hear the trumpet sounding an end to the war. Gance
has beautifully expressed the sense of consciousness slipping away
through manipulation of the image, not, as one might expect, of the
sound track, as a series of dissolves places the trumpeter farther and
farther away on the distant horizon. We soon see that Gilles's imaginings are real. The cease-fire has really come. As the army rejoices,
the Death Patrol is brought back. Ten dead, one dying, one missing.
The patrol will all be buried at Douamont, which they defended for
sixteen months. The priest prays as the rest of the army celebrates.
Then a moaning is heard. Diaz is still alive. Brought back to the
hospital, he is placed in a bed alongside that of François Laurin, the
other survivor, who is dying. Laurin grasps his hand. It is as if his
life flows into Diaz, as if one life is exchanged for another. It is also

symbolic of the special bond that will remain between Diaz and his dead companions.

In a bitterly ironic scene, Gance juxtaposes shots of the dead and of crosses in the cemetery with shots of parades, to the sound of the "Marseillaise" and the "Chant du Départ": "The Republic calls you/ Be prepared to win or die/ A Frenchman should live for Her/ For Her, a Frenchman ought to die." This scene is formally paralleled with Flo's song sequence. Jean Diaz goes to comfort François Laurin's widow. (In the earlier version, it will be remembered, she had been in love with Diaz, but this episode has pretty much disappeared from the sound version.) Diaz then retires to his workshop at Douamont, vowing to work exclusively for the fulfillment of his promise that there will be no more war: "Within me," he states, "is all the force of the dead." Then, in 1938, Diaz returns to work in Chimay's factory, where he succeeds in increasing production. Chimay offers to make him his partner, but Diaz is uninterested. Chimay, a budding politician, gives a speech to his employees, arguing that armaments are indispensable to a strong democracy. The government's motto calls for "a preponderance of power." When Chimay returns from the speech, Diaz, who is reputed never to argue but only to accuse, bursts out, passionately accusing Chimay and others of leading men on the path to war once again: "You laugh cynically at the most beautiful words of all: 'Love one another.'"

Diaz returns to his "family" at Douamont. His room is a monument to his memories; photos of the dead are arranged on the wall in a cruciform pattern. There is a note reminding him that nine million died and seventeen million were wounded in the war. In his visual depiction, Gance therefore transforms this room into an emblem of accusation. Diaz then discovers Flo, who now runs a little café for a decreasing number of visitors to the cemetery. Her lover, Tenant, missing in action, has never been found. In a moving, lyrical scene, Diaz calls the names of the patrol, one by one, equating them with the tumbling wheat and the blowing cornflowers which cover their graves, the forces of life commemorating their death. "How you are alone," he exclaims to them. This lyrical scene foreshadows the more horrible roll call that is to come later.

The next scene is a storm, apocalyptic in its force. The scene is effective in what is not shown. Diaz knocks on Flo's door in the middle of the torrent, his hair white, with fire in his eyes. Is he mad? He goes out into the storm and calls the names of his departed comrades, declaring: "I have almost succeeded!"

We then find Jean Diaz at the Chimay house in Paris. Overwhelmed by his experience of the last scene, he is unconscious of his surroundings. Chimay has sold Jean's invention, a plastic bulletproof shield which Diaz hoped would make war impossible, to the Ministry of National Defense: "In this age we must use every invention. War is inevitable." Chimay has become the leader of a protofascist party. We are presented with a visual and sound montage: Headlines reflect the march toward war; planes, armies, boats are on the move; three tanks suddenly break through the forest and cross a *chemin creux*. Diaz is still immobilized. Finally he sees a plaque awarded to Chimay for the "invention" of steel glass. The plaque transforms itself into a map of Verdun. Diaz is dazed. Where is he? What year is it? He makes his way to the railroad station. A public-address system informs the crowd that gas masks will be supplied to every household and explains how they should be put on babies. With Diaz, we peer at a woman with a baby in the crowd, innocents soon to be victimized by a political situation beyond their control.

The next scene shows Diaz standing before the monument at Verdun. He talks to the tower, whose two lights shine like eyes, transfixing the inventor. It is as if a voice is giving him commands: "I have come. Have I rightly understood. . . . Is it I who is chosen? Is this the moment?" He calls the name of François Laurin, whose life was exchanged for his: "Your sacrifices were in vain. I shall not yield to war. I return to you. Refuse. Help me!" Gance is operating within an essentially animist universe. He shared Jean Epstein's belief that cinema is polytheist and theogenist: "I believe that if one wants to understand," Epstein writes, "how an animal, a plant, a rock can inspire respect, fear, horror, the three sacred feelings, they must be seen living their lives on the screen—mysterious, mute, and strange to human sensibility"[2] Nowhere does Gance better capture the eerie feeling of things becoming beings. Nowhere does Gance better reveal the surreal idealism of his work which sees the world with a nonhuman eye. There is a tracking shot of the cemetery. The names on the graves glow. *"Morts de Verdun, levez-vous. Je vous appelle!"* The camera's movement speeds up. Shots proceed at all angles. "Soldiers of the Great War, I call you. *Soldaten des Weltkriegs. . . ."* A statue is shown with a distorting lens. The stone twists, writhes; it begins to live. We see the storm, birds flying madly, a flower dying. The crosses vanish, dissolving into the cemetery. "My twelve million friends killed in the war, I call you." The dead arise and begin marching. (According to Icart, in the full print they stop planes from flying and armies from marching. The frightened nations of the world ban war and proclaim the Universal Republic. The dead can then return to their cemeteries.)

The people of Douamont are frightened. The crowd is shown at an angle, as if all is out of kilter. Diaz tells them that fear alone can stop them now. They have betrayed their dead. A woman suggests that they burn Diaz. Flo tries to stop them, exclaiming that Diaz is trying to save them from war. Nonetheless, he is put to the flames, just as the marching dead arrive. François Laurin and the dead soldiers carry him off the pyre and the film ends. The Passion of Jean Diaz is over.

The worth, the value, the *intelligence* of this film were not unnoticed at the time. The well-known critic of *Le Temps*, E. Vuillermez, wrote "For the first time, perhaps, a film shows us war without indulgence. In *J'Accuse* we do not find that secret complacency hidden in so many works of the same genre. Abel Gance excommunicates war with a logic and vigor which are not impaired by ideology. It's the cry of the rebel against the blindness of men who too easily resign themselves to new killings."[3] And there can be no doubt that *J'Accuse* has withstood the test of time. It is dated, perhaps, by its decor, but the humanitarian impulse remains convincing; the eerie images of the marching dead at the film's conclusion, the battalion of mutilated war veterans, are unforgettable to the degree that we are both haunted and disturbed by them. Few filmmakers have ever organized images to better effect.

4

The First Symbol of the Seventh Art: *La Roue*

La Roue (completed April 9, 1921, and released in April of 1923) is a unique motion picture, created during a period of profound personal anguish. The tone, evoking suffering and fatality, is set by the opening quotation from Victor Hugo: "Creation is a Great Wheel which does not move without crushing someone." This opening motto is then followed by a visual symphony of image and action. The first image is a close-up of the director's face; superimposed over it is a long shot of trains in motion. In *Prisme* Gance recalls having read "*The Rail* of Hamp some time ago. All that I can remember," he explains, "is that in it there's a remarkable railroad disaster with a real musical composition. I must work in this direction, but also in a larger fashion on the human plane." The "Première Epoque" of *La Roue*—entitled "The Rose of the Rails"—indeed "works in this direction," as promised.

The opening sequence of the film conveys a sense of the power of machines in motion, first showing men and machines in harmony, then—disaster: wheels turning; people "crushed." Perhaps a hint of the power and movement of the film's "Première Epoque" may be suggested by a brief description of the opening montage, for at key points in this film—especially at the outset and, much later, when one of the central characters plunges from the side of Mt. Blanc, his death witnessed by the woman who loves him—Gance comprehends the emotional power of controlled montage to an astonishing degree for 1921. The first montage begins when a shot of a locomotive moving directly toward the camera dissolves to the circular plate on the front of the engine in close-up. Superimposed over this appears the face of Sisif (Sisyphus, the central character of the film, played by Séverin-Mars). Next, a shot of a steaming locomotive moving away from the camera cuts to a masked travelling shot of a single rail on the roadbed. This image then opens up to

79

show rails joining at the switchpoints, as the camera passes over them, a flux of rails joining and parting, repeated three times. Gance then cuts to a shot of the side of a locomotive, with the image in close-up of a wheel superimposed over it, dissolving to a close-up of wheels and drive-rods in motion. This preparatory sequence, establishing the movements of trains from these several perspectives, concludes with a long shot of engines meeting in the railroad yards.

Suddenly—disaster and confusion: cars tilted crazily, in the midst of which Sisif rescues the child Norma, as, in the foreground one notices a locomotive wheel with a chain draped over it, an iconographic suggestion of impeded mechanical motion. Enraged in the turmoil, Sisif races into the control tower and begins to throttle the block operator, whom he apparently holds responsible for the accident, after which he immediately throws the switches that should close off the mainline; but, as we will soon discover, in such a chaotic world nothing can be taken for granted. Gance shows us a close-up of the turned signal-disc along the mainline, then cuts to a close-up of a rose against a rock, followed by a series of shots revealing the wreckage and its victims: a mother who is trying to attend a screaming baby collapses and rolls down an embankment; another woman's body slumps lifelessly through the window of a wrecked passenger-car.

In this misery and confusion, as dazed survivors mill over the rails through the smoke and wreckage, one notices Sisif holding the child Norma. Still in the foreground is the engine wheel, resting upon the switchpoint. All of a sudden, another train approaches; Sisif quickly carries Norma to safety, rushing back immediately in an attempt to clear the wheel from the track. At this point Gance brilliantly organizes a tense montage of intercutting shots: 1) Norma screaming in close-up; 2) the approaching train; 3) Sisif straining to move the wheel; 4) then to a moving shot from the approaching train (shots 3 and 4 are rapidly intercut four times in succession to build tension); to 5) a close-up of instruments in the cab of the approaching locomotive; to 6) a shot from the moving cabin, behind the engineer looking out of his window; to 7) a close shot of wheels and churning drive-rods; to 8) a long shot of stalled passenger cars in the wreckage, as the heads of surviving passengers who hear the approaching danger begin to crane out of the windows; to 9) Sisif in long shot attempting to roll the wheel; to 10) the stalled cars again (19 frames); to 11) shot behind engineer in cab (11 frames); to 12) wrecked cars on a hillside; to 13) a held shot (118 frames) first of the rock and rose isolated by an iris until the image irises out to reveal Norma in center frame, huddled on the ground. The montage is concluded by a forty-two-frame close-up of Norma (in the same position as in shot no. 13).

The effect of this opening in the way it involves the viewer directly in the action is stupefying, and unlike anything that had yet been seen in cinema. The spectacular legacy of the Lumières' approaching engine is increased a thousandfold by this torrent of images in action. And it is only after this hypnotic establishing montage that Gance gives us his first subtitle: "During the night Sisif remembers the Rose of the Rails."

In *Prisme* Gance discusses the genesis of this film and explains his motives for making it:

Less and less I feel the cinema capable of defending its real works, and each day I retreat from my great subjects. The instruments are too imperfect for me to be able to construct my cathedrals of light. Architect, mason, priest, I bend under my tempest of sunlight. . . . A little night to breathe. Let us mount the steps, one by one. I search for some more melodramatic motif and at the same time an eternal subject which can utilize a world made for the cinema, the world of locomotives, of rails, of signals, of smoke. . . . And by way of contrast, a world of snow, of mountain-tops, of solitude; a symphony-in-white following a symphony-in-black. To make catastrophes of feelings and of machines keep pace with one another, each as great as the other, equally elevated in significance; to show the ubiquity of all that beats—a heart and a steam-engine. In direct opposition to theatrical drama, this drama will be created by exteriors, by ambiences which little-by-little disengage the hero. I decide on July 30th, 1919, in the park of the Caux Palace, after a long conversation with my beloved, to execute *La Roue*. With this film I will make use of the true dramatic language of the screen, to wit: the pathos in things brought to the same level as that in men. Since attaining the age of reason I have believed, according to my metaphysic, that Matter is living. The lyric proof remains to be demonstrated.[1]

He goes on to say, "I must maintain the simplicity of an ancient tragedy in its construction." He continues thereafter to work on this tragedy of suffering and solitude with the knowledge that the woman he loves, Ida Danis, has been diagnosed as having a severe case of pulmonary tuberculosis and that her recovery is unlikely. In his sorrow, Gance throws himself into the project: "To work! Let this wheel dredge the river of my sufferings and bring back to me

golden nuggets and diamonds." Resolved, therefore, to climb the
steps one at a time, this would-be architect of "cathedrals of light"
decides to make the film.

La Roue is not Abel Gance's best-known film today; it may be his
most important film historically. This film marks a breakthrough on
a number of levels. Technically, Gance has taken the camera off the
tripod and made it mobile by attaching it to a moving train. But this
innovation is nothing compared with the film's aesthetic and
psychological achievements.

"La Roue, paroxysm of Fatality, is the crossroads of Aeschylean
tragedy, the Latin Fatum, and the Eternal Return of Nietzsche,"
writes Jean Arroy.[2] For Jean Epstein, the Wheel is the first
cinematographic symbol. For Fernand Léger, the film is the first
cinematographic fact. It marks the decisive breaking away of film
from theater. (We assume he had not seen The Birth of a Nation.)
Léger explains that the cinema enables us to see what we had
merely noticed before: "The mere fact of projection of the image
already defines the object, which becomes spectacle." That is the
basis of the new art: "Abel Gance has sensed it perfectly. He has
achieved it; he is the first to have presented it to the public. You will
see moving images presented like a picture, centered on the screen
with a judicious range in the balance of still and moving parts (the
contrast of effects); a still figure on a machine that is moving, a
modulated hand in contrast to a geometric mass, circular forms,
abstract forms, the interplay of curves and straight lines (contrasts of
lines), dazzling, wonderful, a moving geometry that astonishes
you."[3]

Here is a film which brings out the pantheism of Gance, a film in
which the machine, animal, and man are all equally dramatis personae. Sisif is caught between the Wheel of Fatality and his own
obsessions; the wheel is everywhere; we too are caught. Only Sisif's
acceptance of his condition can give him peace; we too are released
by his death from the intolerable weight of his sufferings which
become ours. Léger rightly argues that La Roue operates on three
states: dramatic, emotional, and plastic, and that in the third, the
machine becomes the leading actor. This mechanical element "is
presented to us through an infinite variety of methods, from every
aspect; close-ups, fixed or moving mechanical fragments, projected
at a heightened speed that approaches the state of simultaneity and
that crushes and eliminates the human object, reduces its interest,

pulverizes it."[4] This film is not a film about man's enslavement by mechanical civilization; rather, it uses the machine, epitomized by the train, as the instrument of Fatality, as the blind organ of the Higher Powers of Necessity. Gance ruthlessly examines man's pretensions to freedom and destroys them. Man cannot prevail against the forces of Fatality. Sisif finds consolation only when he accepts the existence of his fatality; he can then die peacefully while his adopted daughter, Norma, joins in the Round Dance at the heights of Mt. Blanc.

Listen to Jean Epstein:

Wheel. The modern martyrs who profess our dogma of hard truths carry it on their foreheads, heavy like an intelligent love. Wheel. On the predestined rails of Chance, good and above all evil, it rolls as long as a heart beats. The cycle of life to death has become so mortifying that it must be forged so as not to be broken. Hope radiates at the center, a prisoner. Wheel. Belt tying the body to the will, desires, like uneasy and feverish foxes in a cage, pursue in a circle. Once born, no one can leave it, and remains as if alone in the world, alone in his wheel at rest, because no one knows the flagrant word which would create a breach of sympathy in the barrier. Wheel. Each is sealed by it in the heart of the other, remaining mute and deaf. While it turns, its timetable of death and oblivion ripens, effacing the faces in the hearts, impressing over and above the seasons and the years, showcases of memories, always something other than what one awaits. Wheels, the bellowing wheels of express trains, how many farewells brush past the stations, stenograms and drawn blinds waddle in their sad night jog. The connecting rods hasten an irrevocable drama, more somber than all Greek tragedy. The departures have fallen due. The cross which turns very quickly takes the form of a wheel. That is why, at the summit of your Calvary, Gance, there is the wheel. By dint of hastening towards death, we have made the rose flower on the cross, the wheel, rose of the cross. More than a symbol, it is a scar, an inflamed sign, fatal like that which incendiaries carry under the left breast.[5]

Man is the victim of a Fatality outside him, but victim alike of the obsessions within. Indeed, they are one. Sisif is pursued, as Elie, his son, is pursued, by an impossible and passionate love, a love which cannot be fulfilled but cannot be forgotten. The Norma who enters their lives, the little girl saved from a train wreck who grows up to be loved by both, cannot belong to either. Sisif cannot tell Norma that she is not his child; Sisif will not tell Elie, his rival, that she is not his sister. The film is very Freudian indeed; its real subject is incest—that greatest love which cannot be allowed. If

Gance has captured the power of *Oedipus Rex*, it is because his drama has dared enter this forbidden country. Gance has fixed on a universal taboo. No one cannot escape the obsession of Sisif. And therefore we are all caught in the archetypical wheel of this drama.

The intensity of *La Roue* is related to the tragic circumstances of its creator's own life. The film is dedicated to his beloved Ida: "Begun on the first day of your illness, I finished it on the day of your death. Once again, 'the edge of wisdom returns against the wise man.' It is really stupefying to see this coincidence, this transposition of Fatality which I draw from nothingness, from my own Fatality."[6]

The tragic Sisif of *La Roue* first appears as a young hero. Two trains move rapidly toward destruction. A switch will not function. In this night scene, Gance establishes the sense of confusion in which everyone is helpless. Then suddenly, a man radiating energy and decision takes charge. Sisif turns a vast wheel to move a switch and avert yet another wreck. "He sees everything. He understands everything. He is everywhere." While bureaucrats try to assess blame, he saves lives. Finding a four-year-old girl, orphaned by the wreck, he brings her home as a sister to his little son Elie. The signalman tells the inspectors that the switch had refused to work. "Far away, beneath the moon, the criminal disk is like a monstrous figure of the apocalypse. It seems to wink its cyclopean eye satanically. . . ." Sisif finds a letter proving that Norma's parents are dead. He destroys it. He sees the signal-disk guarded by two gendarmes. It seems to Sisif as if the disk calls him a child-thief. Sisif returns home to find the children playing with model trains. Their play recapitulates the accident itself. Sisif takes a little doll from out of the toy train wreck. He guesses confusedly that "the Wheel of Life is going to become heavier for him with the weight of Norma's fatality."

The first epoch of the film opens fifteen years later. We see Sisif in a bar, *Les Gueules Noires*. He seems to be thirty years older, his face is ravaged, and unlike many of the other railroad workers, he obviously has been drinking. Asleep in a corner, his back against the window, he looks like a "Christ of the tavern, with the windows of the bistro as his halo." A fortune-teller looks at his palms and lets go of his hand with horror. The ticks and expressions of Sisif's face betray obsession, an impression accentuated by the use of close-ups and sharp contrasts when showing Sisif. Told that another railroad man is interested in his daughter, he attacks the man violently.

Meanwhile Sisif's son Elie, a musical instrument maker, is saddened by the life around him, a sadness suffused by his unconscious love for Norma. Both he and Norma dream about life in the Middle Ages. Each imagines an ideal beloved resembling the other. The love of brother and sister infuriates Sisif, who forbids them to spend time together.

The extent of Sisif's obsession is demonstrated by a powerful scene. Sisif is seated at the table in the evening, working on an invention for which his boss, De Hersan, will get the credit. He bends over a model of a locomotive, then pushes it aside. "Slowly his eyes seek the stairway, fascinated by the insurmountable desire to climb up. Like a sleepwalker, he gets up and climbs each step slowly, as if something held him back, but inexorably, as if something pushed him forward." Suddenly, he shakes off his compulsion and ties a piece of cord across the stairs. Horrified by his own desires, he writes a letter explaining that he is leaving, but falls asleep exhausted. In the morning, Norma and Elie see the letter and prevail upon him to remain. Believing that Sisif's strange behavior is due to poverty, Norma considers responding to De Hersan's offer of marriage, a possibility which horrifies Elie. Sisif's consent results from indiscretion on his part. Desperately in need of a confidant, Sisif tells his story to De Hersan. He evokes their early happiness, and Sisif's subsequent discovery that he was in love with Norma. Flashbacks are shown by means of overexposure, contrasting with the stark composition of the other shots. We observe Norma riding on a swing. As she ascends, Sisif can see her legs. He is beside himself. He draws the curtains, but then can't resist opening them a little bit to see her. It has come to the point where Sisif is afraid to see Norma except when he is blackened with dirt. De Hersan uses this information to blackmail Sisif into accepting his marriage with Norma. Sisif attempts to commit suicide by running himself over with his own train, but Machefer, the fireman, stops it just in time.

Sisif decides to take Norma to the city himself on the express train. Norma arrives with Elie on the platform, but the train is about to leave, and he cannot kiss her. The train passes the famous signal-disk, and its cyclopean eye seems to wink sarcastically. "You smile, you bastard," cries Sisif, "you think she will escape me. No, she will not arrive living between his arms. The Man of the Wheel and the Rose of the Rail are made to die together." Sisif pulls down the throttle all the way. The train speeds forward, and Norma pulls down her curtain. Her face and the smoke of the train are superim-

posed. Gance evokes the sense of speed through rapid cutting, shots
of the rails, etc. Sisif goes through a stop signal, which miraculously
changes at the last moment. Horrified, Machefer seizes the controls
and stops the train. Sisif seems to awaken from a horrible nightmare. Having lost Norma, Sisif attempts to transfer his love to the
engine.

In the second epoch, Elie discovers that Norma was not his sister.
Sisif stood between him and happiness. He remembers bringing his
father back drunk from the bistro, Sisif muttering that he would
drown his obsession in the moon of the well. Sisif, too? They understand that they both loved Norma, and still love her. Their feeling of
love and hate for each other parallels the love-hate relationship of
François Laurin and Jean Diaz in *J'Accuse*. Norma seems to Sisif
like "the center of an inexorable wheel, innocently carrying all
fatalities in its spokes."

Through the negligence of Machefer, Sisif is partly blinded. Fire
is reflected in his eyes. Machefer brings him to his train. It is all
vague, tarnished, mottled. The anguish of Sisif is like that of Beethoven going deaf. The camera work captures the subjective point of
view of Sisif, just as it had done in the stairway scene. When Sisif
discovers that the company plans to take away his train, he is in
agony. His mind's eye is filled with wheels; he hears trains that are
not there, sees signals opening and closing. He goes to his locomotive. "We feel them tied by an accord stronger than necessity:
friendship. It is an extra-human friendship, a fetichist, animist, mystic, mysterious feeling, closed to ordinary human sensibility." Sisif
asks the engine whether it wouldn't prefer death to separation, and
it seems to say yes. Sisif decides to kill himself and the engine. The
engine hits a buffer-stop. When Sisif regains consciousness, the
machine has flattened itself. Its disembowelled smoke-box is filled
with flowers from the field. Heaving a last sigh, the machine seems
to say farewell.

The third epoch takes place on Mt. Blanc. Sisif has been demoted
to being the engineer of the funicular railway. On top of the mountain he lives in a small cabin with Elie and his dog, Toby. He is
losing the rest of his vision. He looks at the light in the simplest
things: his pipe, a glass. Elie is trying to discover the secret of the
violin varnish of Cremona; his success will not bring him happiness,
however. As chance would have it, Norma and De Hersan come to
Mt. Blanc on vacation. Norma sees her father and Elie, who pre-

vents her from calling out Sisif's name. Norma's return exacerbates
Elie's old conflicts with his father, for Sisif senses her return, and
wants her to go away: "Is there a cancer in the family, papa?" Elie
asks. At night there is a tempest on Mt. Blanc. A tree is hit by
lightning and falls into the abyss. De Hersan intercepts a letter from
Elie to Norma, and in a fit of jealousy goes after Elie. In a terrible
fight on the mountain crags, De Hersan is wounded and Elie who
falls, is left hanging on a mountain ledge. De Hersan gets to Sisif's
cabin, and Toby, Sisif, and Norma rush out. Elie is still hanging
desperately from a ledge; "he disappeared with overwhelming instantaneity, but it seemed to Norma that for several interminable
seconds she could see Elie's face with the expression of death inscribed." It was as if he was calling upon her to make a miracle.
Then he falls to his death. Sisif chases Norma away as if she were an
assassin. Norma doesn't understand what fatality has caused her to
bring unhappiness and death to those she loves. She sinks into
unconsciousness. The blind Sisif now begins to understand:

When the moon rises on the glacier in the evening, Sisif is still kneeling
down at the same place. Silent and somber, wild, eyes closed, he listens all
around him as if to an immense and muffled turning of unleashed and
obscure forces.

He knows that one does not resist the high fatal forces of life. He accepts
being the eternal castaway carried by the current, and he thinks that the real
strength of man is not to revolt, but to resign himself.

Thus that inexorable wheel turns, that wheel which placed into the
center of multiple tragic spokes the motionless face of the little girl found
one catastrophic night on the Rail of Life and Death.

On the anniversary of Elie's death, Sisif takes a cross which he has
hewn himself and is led by Toby to the site of his son's death:

From halting-place to halting-place, from station to station, bending under
the enormous burden he bears, he finally arrives at the site of the place
where, a year ago, he was kneeling and where he had passed the whole
night in interminable prayer.[7]

Norma is there too, prematurely aged. She sees that Sisif is blind. It
is a Passion scene, 9,000 feet above sea level. Sisif sits and takes
bread and wine: Norma is Mary Magdalene. She resigns herself not
to follow him.

Sisif has not yet fully accepted fatality. He doesn't want Norma back. In the fourth part, she returns. She sleeps anywhere. He senses her presence, sometimes seeming to accept, at other times lashing out at her with his baton. Finally he accepts her. One day, he speaks to her as if they had just parted the day before. Sisif has finally found peace and serenity. Now that he is blind, he finally can see the light. Accepting his fatality, he is no longer oppressed by it.

The Festival of the Guides arrives. The young people ask Norma to join their dance. We see the round dance circling higher and higher on the slopes of Mt. Blanc. There follows a series of rapid cuts. Sisif drops his model train and his pipe, and falls back in his chair. Smoke forms circles. Toby barks. Sisif's expression is peaceful. The round continues. We see trains, smoke, Toby, clouds. The round dance crosses over Elie's death place. Sisif is seen from the back with the window open. The last shot shows clouds at the peak of Mt. Blanc. Sisif at last has found peace.

The plot of *La Roue* is complex, but its dramatic thrust and impact simple and direct. Make no mistake—the audience suffers with Sisif just as the Christian suffers with its God made Man. Moreover, plot summaries are deceptive. Seemingly complex plots attain sense and direction when the *cinéaste*, like Gance, knows how to integrate them visually. The impact of the first cinematographic symbol is enormous. Everything reminds us of the Wheel: Norma's hat is circular, the window in her room and in Sisif's cabin is circular. Round wheels, round smoke, round dance. We are overwhelmed, we are possessed, we are dominated by this symbolism. The tragedy takes on universal proportions.

The heaviness of obsession, the weight of fatality. There is no room for accident in this film. Everything is pregnant with meaning in this universe where all things are part of a single living continuum. Two children playing repeat the archetypical event of the train wreck; a tree struck by lightning falls to its death in the same place where Elie will fall. Norma bites her handkerchief when she writes her letter of acceptance to De Hersan's proposal; Elie bites his sweater in his last seconds of agony as he tries to hold on to the ledge. Norma stands transfixed after Elie's fall, her hand moving as with a will of its own to her forehead, then tugging slowly at a lock of hair.

There is no escape. The camera will not let us avoid the obsession in Sisif's face in close-up. We see the world through Sisif's eyes.

The mottled engine of a half-blind man. The stairway leading to the primal crime. Not a thought is unrevealed. Through superimposition we see what each thinks. Sisif sees the smoke of the engine over the rails on which he plans to destroy Norma and himself, and her face is superimposed on that smoke. The imaginings of Norma when she first imagines marrying De Hersan form six little balloons around his image: jewels, a car, etc. Things are superimposed because nothing exists independently of anything else. All is living, but all lives under the sign of the same Fatality. There is an extraordinary maturity in this film: Sisif accepts his fate in the same way that Prospero overcomes his feelings at the end of *The Tempest* and accepts things as they are.

If the audience is sucked into the movements of the film, it is partly because Gance has discovered the use of musical rhythms in the visual:

> At the moment in *La Roue* when the locomotive is thrown by Sisif on the buffer-stop, I was able to alternate the images like verse: Eight—four, eight—four, eight—four, four—two, four—two. One succeeds thus in obtaining a true rhythm. Later, we shall succeed in composing perfect cinematographic poems with rimes that will fall at regular intervals, like drops, by recalls of images. [8]

Despite the metaphysical scope of his films, Gance ever remains the disciple of Horace who knows how to polish his cinematic verses.

Gance makes extensive use of quotations from famous authors throughout the film. This overly literary quality was strongly criticized by René Clair. Clair felt that the film was encumbered by its "improbable situations, superficial psychology" typical of Romantic drama. "Oh, if Mr. Abel Gance would only give up making locomotives say yes and no, lending a railroad engineer the thoughts of a hero of antiquity, and quoting his favorite authors! . . . Oh, if he were willing to give up literature and place his trust in the cinema!"[9] Clair is making two points. The first, a criticism of the plethora of literary citations, was explained by Gance in an interview as a means of getting acceptance for his new symbol by a public which might not otherwise choose to understand.[10] No one can pretend that these quotations strengthen the visual element of the film, which might well have been allowed to stand on its own! The second point is really the objection of an essentially social filmmaker, a kind of realist, against the pantheism and animism inherent in *La Roue*.

Gance is not simply making his locomotives say yes and no for effect. Clair's objection reflects a basic philosophic difference dividing them. But Clair is far from denying the genius, the revolutionary quality of this film. He expresses himself in a way similar to Léger:

> As I see it, the real subject of the film is not its odd plot, but a train, tracks, signals, puffs of smoke, clouds. From these great visual themes Gance has drawn splendid developments. We had already seen trains moving along tracks at a velocity heightened by the obliging movie camera, but we had not yet felt ourselves absorbed—orchestra, auditorium, and everything around us—by the screen as by a whirlpool. . . . The catastrophe at the beginning of the film, the first accident Sisif tries to cause, the ascent of the cable car into the mountains, the death of Elie, the bringing down of his body, the round dance of the mountaineers, and that grandiose ending amidst veils of clouds: these are sublime lyrical compositions that owe nothing to the other arts.[11]

Gance himself did not feel that he had produced a finished work of art, or that such a work was yet possible:

> I think that I can permit myself to say that there are certain close-ups of Séverin-Mars in *La Roue* which were well done and shall not stir, and which won't be surpassed for fifty years. But this is only a corner of the mosaic. There would be art if this piece were set down in the great mosaic from which it could not be detached without compromising the perfect harmony of the whole. It's not that way. The great mosaic doesn't exist. The fragment is only a fragment.[12]

Gance admits the existence of romantic, repetitious, and childish elements in *La Roue*, and says that he would have preferred to concentrate on the moments of paroxysm, of intensity. The public, however, had to be led forward step by step. It is not Gance's fault if the film still seems avant-garde. Gance was ready to move forward, but the film-businessmen were not so anxious.

La Roue marks a step toward the realization of the dream of creating a Seventh Art which would subsume all the others. Gance was assisted by the famous writer Blaise Cendrars, who in turn was assisted by Fernand Léger, the great modern artist. The composer Honegger was charged with preparing a musical score. Honegger wrote in the *Gazette des Sept Arts* (January 25, 1923) that he sought "an absolute correspondence between the animating spirit of a fragment of the film and its *musical rhythmic confirmation.*"

The sluices of the imagination had been opened. The Seventh Art had started. A cinematographical language was in the process of being created. And Gance had just begun. Despite the achievements of *J'Accuse* and *La Roue*, *Napoléon* was still ahead of him.

5

The Hero As Artist: *Napoléon*

A STUDY OF THE FILMS of Abel Gance, individually or collectively, cannot ignore the sources which influenced the filmmaker and from which he drew his inspiration. His projected biography of Columbus, for example, clearly derives in part from Salvador de Madariaga; his treatment of Beethoven was influenced by the artistic theories of Ricciotto Canudo, whom he knew; likewise, his epic biography of Napoleon, his only major film based on a nontragic narrative development, derives from his close friend Elie Faure's book on Napoleon, which views France's great national hero as an artist: "From the point of view of art, everything about him becomes clear. He was a poet of action. That is all. . . . Like all artists, he was capable of making mistakes in his art; and from the moral angle these are regarded as crimes. But his work, as a whole, is as astonishing as any ever conceived by an artist."[1]

In his film Gance chooses to ignore the "mistakes" in Napoleon's art. He does not want to emphasize the moral implications of the later "crimes." Gance does seize upon the idea of Napoleon as artist, however, and in this respect his treatment can be seen as a cinematic *Künstlerroman*. Faure's biography, to be sure, is not Gance's *only* source; but Faure's notion of the Hero is central to Gance's vision of Napoleon in his historical epoch. Beyond this, Faure's notion of artistic invention applies equally well to his friend Abel Gance as to the artist Napoleon: "The Creator invents nothing. He takes the materials which present themselves and combines them according to his imagination."[2]

Napoléon (completed in 1926, released in Paris, April 7, 1927) may be Abel Gance's greatest film; it is certainly his most famous. And yet, ironically, it is very much different in certain fundamental ways from his other most important works. *J'Accuse, La Roue,* and *Beethoven* are all "tragic" in that they end with the death or the

93

madness of their protagonists. *Napoléon,* on the other hand, ends at the high point of General Bonaparte's career with his first great victories as General of the Army of Italy. To be sure, the end of Napoleon's life may be considered "tragic," but since the film deals only with Bonaparte before he becomes Napoleon, the Emperor, this tragic dimension is only suggested in Gance's filmed biography.

In Gance's other films, there is a kind of marriage between a Hegelian ideal of the hero in history and a kind of Christian morality. In this film, the hero is a man of action who seems to transcend any moral categories. Indeed, Gance's characterization of Napoleon calls to mind Elie Faure's statement: "From the point of view of morality he is indefensible. Indeed, he is incomprehensible. In actual fact, he violated the law, he killed, he sowed vengeance and death. Yet he made the law, he tracked crime to its source and crushed it, he established order everywhere. He was an assassin; he was also a redresser of wrongs. As an ordinary person, he would have deserved to be hanged. But in his supreme position he was unsullied; he distributed rewards and punishments with a firm hand. He was a monster—double-faced. Like all of us perhaps. In any case, like God."[3]

Of course, there are other influences at work here as well. Abel Gance's conception of history, for example, is very close to that of Plutarch: "I think sufficiently like Plutarch that the utility of the descriptive historian is contestable. But is that the limit of [the historian's] role? Isn't it his mission, in the calm of his study, sheltered from the noise and details which lead the spirit astray, to clarify and to show the events in a light which allows them to illuminate each other, drawing the deductions which the great leaders themselves never suspected and which, consequently, will serve to teach other leaders?"[4]

History is thus not merely a concatenation of events without sense: beneath the confusing sea of facts there is a meaning. All historians tend to focus on what is "really important." The difference between most historians and Gance, however, is that this extreme idealist looks at things from a very different direction. It is not common, for example, to ascribe Bonaparte's motivation to a desire for the Universal Republic. But for Gance, Napoleon's unfulfilled hopes for such a republic are significant as a precursor of things to come. Socialist historians may give Babeuf's Conspiracy of the Equals or the Commune of 1871 undue importance because they see them as precursors of the inevitable unfolding of history. The difference is, perhaps, that few historians can be as opportunistic with regard to their sources as Gance is in this film. Gance chooses what fits in with his vision: if the facts do not fit the theory, so much the worse for the facts. Thus, Gance's historical characters are often distorted—and yet, his intuitive genius often attaches itself to things that professional historians may fail to grasp. In such cases, the well-informed artistic imagination transports him to a parallel truth.

In the course of an article appearing in *Paris-Soir*, Gance explained his own conception of Napoleon, which was, in truth, an interpretation:

After much reading and research, I conceived Napoleon as a man who did not absolutely detest war, but who is dragged into it by a powerful mesh of circumstance and who tries constantly but vainly to stop it, because it is the black spot on all his horizons. After Marengo, war becomes his fatality. He does everything he can to avoid it, but he is obliged to submit to it; that's his drama.

Napoleon is the perpetual conflict between the great revolutionary who wants the revolution in peace and who makes war in the fallacious hope of establishing a definitive peace.

He is a man whose arms are not strong enough to channel something greater than he: the Revolution. An admirable human will. But the brain is greater than the heart. His greatest fault is to have made his relatives Kings; he loved them, but with too small a heart, and Napoleon partly falsified his destiny by not being more than the *grand bourgeois* of his caste, whereas he was born to be the great man of the Revolution.[5]

This four-and-one-half-hour film marks one of the truly remarkable moments in the history of the cinema. Although *Napoléon* is certainly a long film, the record for sheer length is of course held by von Stroheim's *Greed;* unlike *Greed,* however, almost all of the original footage of *Napoléon is* still extant, thanks to the efforts of Kevin Brownlow and others. Surely no biographical film of such scope had ever been so elaborately attempted. And, as stated above, it only focuses on a part of Napoleon's career, from early childhood up to his Italian campaign, as he is forced by Destiny toward "Greatness," beyond which point Fatality takes over. The view Gance presents of Napoleon is a romanticized vision of the "great man" theory of history, wrought after the fashion of a *Bildungsroman:* he is possessed of a superhuman, almost supernatural force that shows forth even when he is still a child, organizing a snowball fight at school. (This episode derives from Louis Antoine Fauvelet de Bourrienne's *Memoirs of Napoleon Bonaparte*.) In this sequence, he is presented as a general-in-miniature; in tactics and strategy as in bearing and demeanor, the boy Napoleon (played by Vladimir Roudenko), as Gance suggests, is truly father of the man. The opposing team (or "army") loads its snowballs with rocks. Struck by one of these, hurt, angered, but still undaunted, Napoleon charges his opponents singlehandedly, seeks out and finds the offenders, and thrashes them. This early "victory" is given a metaphorical significance, for what happens in this childhood encounter is intended to foreshadow later events. To capture the confusion of the fight effectively, Gance liberates his camera, making it a portable instrument that can be carried into the thick of the fighting. (For the chase sequence in Corsica much later in the film, Gance mounted the camera on horseback, according to Jean Arroy, and, of course, to capture the turmoil of the storm sequence in the Convention Hall Gance mounted the camera on a "great iron pendulum" that could be oscillated in all directions.) In his camera technique, Gance therefore appears to be at least thirty years ahead of his time, but this is nothing unusual in the career of Abel Gance.

Some may be tempted to consider the snowball-fight sequence at Brienne a popularized contrivance, if not a flight of fancy. But Gance has his inspiration on good authority, as the following passage from the *Memoirs of Napoleon Bonaparte* demonstrates:

During the winter of 1783–4, so memorable for heavy falls of snow, Napoleon was greatly at a loss for those retired walks and outdoor recreations in which he used to take much delight. He had no alternative but to mingle with his comrades, and, for exercise, to walk with them up and down a spacious hall. Napoleon, weary of his monotonous promenade, told his comrades that he thought they might amuse themselves better with the snow, in the great courtyard, if they would get shovels and make hornworks, dig trenches, raise parapets, cavaliers, etc. "This being done," said he, "we may divide ourselves into sections, form a siege, and I will undertake to direct the attacks." The proposal, which was received with enthusiasm, was immediately put into execution. This little sham war was carried on for the space of a fortnight, and did not cease until a quantity of gravel and small stones having got mixed with the snow of which we made our bullets, many of the combatants, besiegers as well as besieged, were seriously wounded.[6]

The *Memoirs* go on to observe that Napoleon was not much liked by his comrades at Brienne, and that he was noted for his "piercing and scrutinizing glance"—further details that are used in Gance's filmed biography.

There are still other details from Napoleon's childhood that are expanded into metaphorical significance, for much time is spent in showing the unusual development of an extraordinary young man, the growth of this "poet of action." Gance's method is essentially poetical and visionary and not merely historical and biographical. Gance's Napoleon, for example, has a pet eagle. The boys whose foul play he has discovered in the snowball fight attempt to get back at him by releasing the eagle from its cage as Napoleon goes to fetch its food. Upon his return, Napoleon finds an empty cage, then furiously marches to the dormitory, where he interrogates each and every boy. No one admits to having released the eagle. Consequently, Napoleon judges them all guilty and attempts to punish his schoolmates by fighting them all at the same time. Thus begins the pillow-fight sequence that surely influenced Jean Vigo in *Zero for Conduct*. To capture the confusion of this scene, Gance uses numerous superimpositions, and also a split-screen technique that divides the frame into six rectangles, each representing separate actions. Additional shots are then superimposed over these split images, as the viewers' visual sense is assaulted by multiplying images of action. This sequence ends as school authorities stop the fight, and Napoleon is put outside the school door as punishment. At this point, then, the eagle returns to its master. The association between Napoleon and the eagle is therefore established early; it returns time and again later in the film—especially in the tryptich montage at the very end, when the head of the eagle appears in the center frame and its fluttering wings, suggesting flight, dominate the supporting frames.

Symbolic touches like this are frequent in the film, but these are perfectly in keeping with Gance's romanticized treatment of the greatest of French heroes. Upon his return to Corsica later in the film, for example, Napoleon advocates the alliance of that island with France rather than with Spain, Italy, or England. His enemies arrange to have a price put on his head. Consequently, Napoleon must escape Corsica; but he first stops to confound the island's governors and to rescue the maligned flag of France. He is pursued

Top: Vladimir Roudenko as young Bonaparte, with his pet eagle at Brienne.
Bottom: The boy Napoleon at Brienne, during a geography lesson about islands—
Corsica, Sicily, Elba, and St. Helena.

Top: The snowball fight at Brienne.
Bottom: Dieudonné as Napoleon, in his study, preparing his campaign.

on horseback, but reaches the sea and appropriates a boat. It has no sail, so Napoleon quickly rigs the Tricolor, letting the winds of destiny unfurl his flag, which helps to carry him back to France. The symbolic overtones are rather heavy here but surprisingly effective nonetheless, a fine visualization of his political sympathies.

Abel Gance constantly gives us clues to foreshadow and anticipate the appeal and charisma, the energy and intelligence, the mystery and enigma of the mature Napoleon (strikingly played by Albert Dieudonné). One is stunned by the power of his visual metaphors. Napoleon on his boat encounters rough seas that become a tempest. Intercut with this development is a tempestuous meeting at the Convention in Paris. Gance first gives us a shot of the sea, waves rippling and shimmering, alive with light. This image is so beautiful and striking that it sticks in the mind (as it must) until shortly thereafter we see a sea of faces at the Convention, each face moving ever so slightly, like the caps of the rippling waves. The storm develops, and the camera comes in close at sea, riding the waterline as the waves billow toward it. Close-ups of waves are intercut with close-ups of faces, further enforcing the association. The camera floats and is carried rhythmically at sea; meanwhile, the camera at the Convention, mounted on a pendulum, swings back and forth in a descending arc over the turbulent crowd. The pendulum swing of the Revolution is complemented by the pendulum swing of the camera as camera movement itself becomes a metaphor for Revolution. Thus twin forces are at work in Nature, as the savior of the Revolution struggles with the force that will ultimately and inevitably carry him to his destiny.

Napoleon's destiny as visualized by Gance literally shines through the hero's eyes. For example, when Napoleon is in Corsica, tracked down by all factions, he appears as if from nowhere at a Corsican inn. Pozzo di Borgo had just cried out: "Our country is England with Paoli: Death to Bonaparte!" Bonaparte gets up on a chair and says with authority: "Our country is France with Bonaparte." These people, all his enemies, are shocked—and immobilized. Bonaparte holds them, transfixed and immobilized, hypnotized by that gleam in his eye. A similar situation occurs later. When he arrives to take command of the army of Italy, Bonaparte meets with the antagonism of its other generals, who resent the fact that an outsider has been given the command. They prepare to defy Napoleon by refusing to stand on his arrival or to uncover. When he arrives, Bonaparte stares at them. One after another, drawn by the magnetism of his eye, they stand up, and, one after another, they uncover. Napoleon has won his command; now he can organize his army and win the war itself.

The film ends with Napoleon in Italy, on the threshold of his greatness. We know his horizons will expand; and, at that very moment, the visual horizons *do* expand, as the frame opens up and we see the panorama of the Italian landscape and the panorama of battle. It is a glorious moment, a perfect wedding of content and technique, of substance and style. Even so, the Polyvision approach becomes even more complex as three separate but concurrent montage sequences explode upon the three screens. Once again the unexpected happens as the triptych panels are bathed in color. The center panel, presenting an heroic close-up of Napoleon, remains in black-and-white, with white tones predominating. Meanwhile, the left panel tints red, and the right panel tints blue. All of a sudden, then, the triptych, still presenting Napoleon and the images of his victory, is transformed into a gigantic Tricolor flag, emblematic at once of the man and his destiny and the nation and its destiny. The cinematic effect, though Romantic, chauvinistic, and, perhaps, heavyhanded, is still magnificent and overpowering. The full effect, which is emotional and sensory, simply defies verbal description. There is nothing quite like it in the history of cinema.

Gance's *Napoléon* is notable for its pyrotechnical accomplishment—for its dynamic editing, its innovative camera movement, its daring use of superimposed images (many more in some instances than any single viewer would be capable of separating), and, finally, for that experiment which Gance called "Polyvision," the precursor of Cinerama, which Gance patented in 1926. Almost equally important, however, is his unique visualization of metaphor. The *"double tempête"* with its parallel editing of the storm at sea and the storm at the Convention is a remarkable achievement. Kevin Brownlow has pointed out that this treatment was inspired by Victor Hugo's simile: "To be a member of the Convention," according to Hugo, "is like being a wave of the ocean."[7] Gance takes this comparison and expands it into a cinematic conceit: parallel storms, the Convention in chaos, while a pantheistic force drives through one storm the force that will quell the other. Gance's vision of Napoleon is ambiguous, touched with the supernatural, expanded into metaphysical proportions. Gance has described his hero as "a

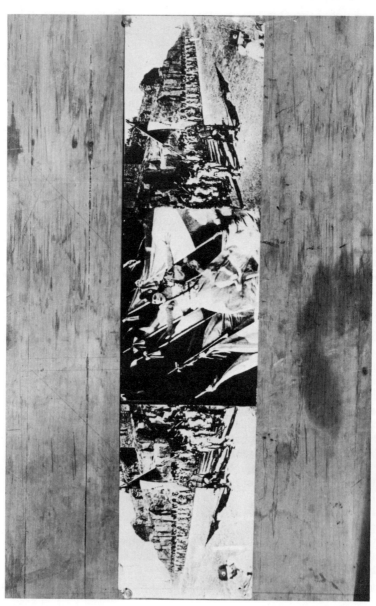

Gance's penchant for national iconography is demonstrated by this triptych from the conclusion of *Napoléon*. On either side of the Spirit of France are reversed images of Napoleon reviewing his troops readied for the Italian campaign.

paroxysm in his epoch, which was also a paroxysm in Time. General Bonaparte is at the periphery of a maelstrom, a lucid observer, while the Emperor is in the whirlpool; he is caught there, and his personal control is abolished."[8] Gance elaborates further: "Bonaparte is not carried by this current. He looks, he observes: he is the master of his destiny. He can brake if he wants. Napoleon no longer can. He no longer has the time or the means. He is in the abyss; he can no longer stop himself; he is obliged to go where fatality pushes him: that's his tragedy which I'm going to try to compose with the music of light."

Gance succeeds in visualizing the supernatural force that drives his protagonist. His eyes burn, ignited by the fires of genius that are kindled in the very core of his being. As in all of Gance's important films, there is an autobiographical element at work here. Gance presents Napoleon as a kind of political artist. In retrospect, the film appears to be a kind of biographical metaphor and an ironic commentary, perhaps, about the workings of fate upon creative energy. In the film Gance takes Napoleon as far as he can go—to the apex of his Republican career; likewise, the film took Gance as far as he could go. There would seem to be a moral here: a genius cannot succeed too brilliantly, for the seeds of his own destruction are sown by that very success. A genius cannot be too far ahead of his times, for the times themselves will ultimately defeat him. The herd will not be led beyond the horizon it views with its own limited vision.

Another example of supernatural foreshadowing is present in this film: at school a geography lesson early in Napoleon's life has a mysterious effect on the young boy. The teacher speaks facetiously of Corsica, where "the people are half civilized," angering Napoleon. Then he draws the outline of St. Helena on the blackboard. The boy stares at it, transfixed, as though inner voices are telling him of his destiny and his ultimate ten-year exile there. Much later, after the tempest at sea, Napoleon is rescued from his rowboat by a French ship. His family conveniently happens to be on board. Concurrently, an English ship spots the French vessel and a young officer named Nelson wants to scuttle her. His commanding officer prevents his taking such action, however, ironically stating that to do so would be a waste of ammunition, time, and effort. This vignette closes with a long shot of Napoleon heroically posed by the mast.

Further coincidences abound, deriving, one supposes, from

legend. Both Napoleon and Josephine de Beauharnais are being held in prison. Both of their dossiers are randomly picked up from a batch of three hundred to be processed for immediate execution. Two clerks, next to one another, independently pick out these two dossiers and proceed to eat the documents, saving both Napoleon and Josephine from certain death. Upon their release, the two meet again at a "Victims' Ball," a bizarre affair that constantly threatens to turn into an orgy but does not, so long as Napoleon and Josephine are present. In the process of winning Josephine, Napoleon competes with General Hoche (Pierre Batcheff). This competition for Josephine's affection effectively adds dramatic tension to the film. Gance is not above manipulating such elements to sustain human interest in his film.

There are many celebrated and marvelous sequences in this film—too many, indeed, to analyze them all. The death scene of Marat, for example, is beautifully done. The composition is such that it approximates the famous David painting. This treatment calls to mind Rossellini's similar tableaux in *The Rise to Power of Louis XIV*. The chase scene in Corsica, in which Bonaparte eludes all his enemies and steals the French flag from Paoli and his clan (saying, "I am taking it away. It is too great for you."), demonstrates a remarkable use of the moving camera, mounted here on Bonaparte's horse. Another example is the taking of the "Little Gibraltar" at the battle of Toulon, at which time Napoleon coins the famous phrase, "Impossible is not a French word."

Dramatic irony runs through the entire film. Working in an obscure post in the topographical bureau of the army, Bonaparte draws up a map for the Italian campaign. It is turned down, with the comment: "These are the plans of a madman. Let the person who wrote them come to execute them himself." Bonaparte pastes the map to his window to cover up a hole. Several years later, named General of the Army of Italy, he takes it down and uses it to win the campaign. Further irony is attained by the introduction into various historical scenes of famous or infamous people. Thus, the Marquis de Sade pops up on one occasion. In the prologue at Brienne, it is Pichegru, one of the faculty, who tells Bonaparte that he will go far. Pichegru, of course, will go far as well. He became one of the leading generals of the French Revolution, but later ended up leading a royalist conspiracy against Napoleon.

The French critic Georges Sadoul writes that Gance "caricatured both Napoleon (of whom Gance was a great admirer) and the Revolution (which he abhorred)."9 The statement is interesting, but, alas, false, as any person who has seen the film should know. Although Gance clearly condemned the excesses of the Revolution, which he does not hesitate to depict, he stresses its positive points, its greatness. How can one forget, for example, the great scene at the Cordeliers Club in which Danton introduces Rouget de Lisle and teaches the crowd the words to the "Marseillaise"? Jean Arroy describes the impact of this scene: "Here life is not learned, repeated, reconstructed by approximation and by formidable effort, but seized living, true, and real, recorded in small fragments whose orchestrated synthesis, one of the most remarkable and intensely expressive, shall compose the most powerful paroxysm of collective expression of a crowd ever shown on the screen."10 In order to create the right atmosphere, Gance made his actors sing the "Marseillaise" twelve times in succession before filming it. This is hardly evidence of a man who abhorred the French Revolution.

Gance makes an even more explicit apologia for the French Revolution in the great scene depicting the advent of Thermidor at the Convention. The members have turned against Robespierre and St. Just. Robespierre tries vainly to get the floor. One member cries out, "The blood of Danton chokes you!" But St. Just (played by Abel Gance himself), in the descriptive words of the scenario,

bounds up to the tribune like a wounded tiger and cries: "JACKALS!" His apostrophe is stupefying. They are quiet. They listen. . . . He, usually so calm, so much a master of himself, is uplifted by a mad lyricism. . . . "YES, WE HAD TO HAVE VICTIMS. BUT ISN'T THE REVOLUTION A GREAT LIGHTHOUSE, ILLUMINATED ON TOMBS?" The crowd is silent. St. Just continues to speak. . . . "THE TERROR HAS PARTLY DESTROYED THE MEANING OF THE REVOLUTION, BUT IT IS NEVERTHELESS THROUGH US THAT THERE SHALL BE LIBERTY IN THE WORLD! CERTAINLY I ADMIT OUR WEAKNESSES. THE EXERCISE OF THE TERROR HAS BLUNTED CRIME AS STRONG LIQUORS BLUNT THE PALATE." [*The script here indicates a thirty-second montage, a series of seven repeated images showing the excesses of the Revolution*] "BUT DO YOU FORGET THAT DURING THIS TIME WE HAVE FORGED A FRANCE ENTIRELY NEW AND READY TO LIVE? . . . 12,000 DECREES, OF WHICH TWO-THIRDS WERE FOR HUMANE GOALS? . . . YOU CAN NOW SCATTER OUR LIMBS TO THE FOUR WINDS: REPUBLICS WILL SURGE FORTH FROM THEM!" The convention is stupefied. It does not know what side to take.

St. Just descends and embraces Robespierre. As they are about to leave, the deputies, full of hate, scream "Death!" St. Just turns around and says: "I FEEL CONTEMPT FOR THE DUST OF WHICH I AM COMPOSED AND WHICH SPEAKS TO YOU. I GIVE MYSELF TO YOU!" One spectator remarks: "THEY ARE TOO GREAT FOR US!"

For Gance, Napoleon is meant to be the continuator of the French Revolution in its positive aspects. His mission is to spread the French Revolution to the rest of the world and at the same time repress its excesses. Gance makes this clear through another famous scene in the film, when Bonaparte, named Commander of the Army of Italy, goes into the empty convention hall and is confronted by the ghosts of the Convention. He looks around him. Is it an illusion? The room is peopled with phantoms which become increasingly visible but remain diaphanous. We see the gigantic shades of such men as Danton, Marat, St. Just, and Robespierre:

We are struck by how death stifling their passions has cemented their ideas and that cohesion, that visible fraternity of the great shades which devoured themselves while living. Danton says to Bonaparte: "LISTEN, BONA-PARTE: THE FRENCH REVOLUTION IS GOING TO SPEAK TO YOU." Robespierre asks him: "WE HAVE UNDERSTOOD THAT THE REVOLUTION CANNOT PROSPER WITHOUT A STRONG AUTHOR-ITY. DO YOU WANT TO BE THE LEADER?" Bonaparte shakes his head, yes. St. Just gets up and says: "IF THE REVOLUTION DOES NOT EXTEND ITSELF OUTSIDE OF OUR FRONTIERS, IT WILL DIE IN PLACE. DO YOU WANT TO CARRY ALONG EUROPE?" Yes. "WHAT ARE YOUR PLANS, BONAPARTE?" asks Marat. "THE LIBERATION OF ENSLAVED PEOPLES, THE FUSION OF GREAT EUROPEAN INTERESTS, THE SUPPRESSION OF FRONTIERS, AND *THE UNIV-ERSAL REPUBLIC*. EUROPE SOON OUGHT TO BE BUT ONE PEOPLE, AND EACH PERSON, WHEREVER HE TRAVELS, SHALL ALWAYS FIND HIMSELF IN THE COMMON COUNTRY. TO ATTAIN THIS SACRED GOAL, MANY WARS SHALL BE NECESSARY. BUT I CRY OUT HERE FOR POSTERITY: ONE DAY VICTORIES SHALL BE ACCOMPLISHED   WITHOUT   CANNONS   AND   WITHOUT BAYONETS." Danton takes Napoleon by the hand. "IF ONE DAY," Danton says to him, "YOU FORGET THAT YOU ARE THE DIRECT IN-HERITOR OF THE FRENCH REVOLUTION, WE SHALL ALL VIO-LENTLY TURN AGAINST YOU."[11]

The scene ends with the dead singing the second stanza of the "Marseillaise," recalling the previous scene at the Cordeliers.

A few words are in order about Abel Gance's choosing for himself the role of St. Just. We believe the reason is clear enough. St. Just is the prophet of the Revolution, and yet he is incapable of leading real events as far as his prophecy extends. Thus it is Napoleon who must carry the French Revolution to its final stage of development. Perhaps this is related to Gance's treatment of St. Just as reflecting a peculiar hermaphroditic tendency. For Gance, hermaphroditism represents a desire to go beyond oneself. Gance discusses this idea in *Prisme:*

I find this explanation, which falls under the force of the axiom: desire creates the need, the need creates the function, the function creates the organ. By dint of wanting to leave the self because one has travelled too much within, one seeks something other than what one is, and that's the direct road to inversion, conscious or not. Man's curiosity of female plea- sure, woman's curiosity of male pleasure, this reversal of the values which always begins through the senses in civilizations at their apogee, already brings about undeniable physiological results. And the number of an- drogynes whose haircut and costume make it difficult to specify is already great. We shall come in "X" generations to the total hermaphroditism of which Maimonides spoke in 1160 when he wrote: "It must be understood that Adam and Eve were created together, united, back to back: understand well how it was clearly said that they were in some sense two, and yet that they formed only one. How strong is the ignorance of those who don't understand that at the bottom of all that there is necessarily an idea."

Biologically, even old Plutarch didn't risk contradiction when he affirmed: "By persistent effort that which is contrary to Nature can become stronger than Nature itself." Who will win, Sparta or Athens?[12]

Interestingly enough, this characterization of St. Just brings to mind the characterization of Jean Novalic in *La Fin du Monde.* Jean Novalic, too, was a prophet, and he too required someone stronger than himself to implement his prophecies. Can it be coincidental, then, that both the role of St. Just and the role of Novalic are played by Abel Gance? Did Abel Gance see himself as a kind of John the Baptist of the cinema?

Finally, if anything is lacking in Abel Gance, it is perhaps the inspiration of the Comic Muse. Canudo had rightly deplored Gance's efforts at humor several years before; the criticism is still valid with reference to *Napoléon.* The scene in which Tristan Fleury eats the contents of Bonaparte's dossier in the office of the public prosecutor, Fouquier-Tinville, for example, is not a high point of the film. Nor is Gance, alas, always particularly gifted in handling romantic encounters. One must conclude that the scenes of Bonaparte's courtship of Josephine are not very humorous when they are meant to be humorous; and at other times they are sentimental and overdone. Bonaparte was certainly ill at ease in his romantic circumstances; Gance's treatment of them is no more fortunate.

Napoléon, then, is a film of some considerable thought and substance. It is epic cinema on a grand scale, spectacular and overwhelming in its impact. It can also be viewed as a sort of national enterprise, since the pride of the French nation is linked to the person of Napoleon. According to Jean Arroy, the idea of filming *Napoléon* first occurred to Gance in 1921, at which time he was in New York, accompanied by Max Linder; on this visit, M. Gance met D. W. Griffith, who also had a similar project in mind. Mr. Griffith, however, "considered it his duty to yield before the man who made *J'Accuse,* and renounced forever his scheme to make the epic."[13] Having won the project, Gance went into a period of intellectual preparation and is reputed to have read hundreds of books dealing with the Emperor and his life. Production expenses must also have been high: 8,000 costumes were manufactured, 4,000 guns, 60 cannon; meanwhile, the streets of old Paris were recreated at the studio at Billancourt. Michel, the symbolic eagle, was obtained through the great Hagenbeck menageries of Hamburg; Arroy reports that the eagle, blinded and burned by the arc lamps, "had to sacrifice himself to art" in order to "gain his mark as a film star."

At the time *Napoléon* was in production, Gance himself described the experience of making the film in transcendental terms: "Every day curious people from all worlds come to the studio in which *Napoléon* is being shot. Entering with smiles on their faces and joking, as if they were in a music hall, they leave most often serious and thoughtful, not to say meditative, as if some hidden god had suddenly opened a golden door in front of them. They have just witnessed in close proximity how a drama is created, calling forth more pain and suffering than reality itself brings into our houses. They have seen how the eyes become rose-windows, stained glass behind which souls burn and blaze, how the 'close-up's' suddenly become great organs of emotion, and how, within a studio, one can, with faith, make a veritable cathedral of light!"[14]

Yet *Napoléon* is mainly remembered for its advanced technology.

Triple-screen panorama of Napoleon overlooking his encamped army.

Fortunately, a number of talents meet in the person of Abel Gance. He is at once a poet, philosopher, and technician. As an artist, he needed the means to express himself precisely the way his vision deemed necessary; as an inventor and technician, he was capable of discovering those means. But it must be stressed that the technology he considered only as an expedient means toward an artistic end. As Gance has explained, "I am an inventor by necessity. Since I don't have the means, I am obliged to find formulas permitting me to express myself. I was far from imagining that I would have been given the gold medal for inventions because my only merit has been finding those things which I absolutely needed. The function creates the organ. How could I have progressed without that?"[15]

Thus "Polyvision" was created, the perfect technological metaphor for illuminating the career of Napoleon Bonaparte, as the dimensions of the ordinary screen are spectacularly expanded to fit the dimensions of this extraordinary man. Gance himself matter-of-factly describes the success of this experiment: "I first put into operation in 1925 my idea of 1922 of constructing a large screen by a combination of three cameras. An apparatus was constructed in three weeks with André Debrie. We burst this first visual atomic bomb in my *Napoléon* at the Paris Opéra on a screen more than twenty yards long. Its success was considerable."[16]

But even though the success was real and "considerable," it was not destined to become the fashion. Gance's technological advances required special screening facilities. Moreover, sound rather than Polyvision was to become the dominant commercial trend. Gance was simply too far ahead of his time, too advanced in his schemes. At least three more decades were to pass before the cinema managers were ready for and receptive to the innovation Abel Gance had pioneered in the middle twenties.

Gance did not lose interest in *Napoléon*, however. In 1934 he attempted a sound version of the film, using most of the original sequences. Since Gance had directed his actors to read historic speeches in the first version, lip synchronization was no problem here.

In 1960, Gance returned to the Napoleon theme with the production of *Austerlitz*. The film covers the story of Napoleon from the Peace of Amiens (1802) until the battle of Austerlitz (December 1805). The Napoleon of this film is no longer the Republican General, but the imperious First Consul about to become Emperor.

Despite his outward strength, he is beginning to lose control over the situation. He is influenced by his family, by his ministers (especially the insidious Talleyrand); he relies more and more on police-state tactics and espionage. His intuition fails him, leading to tragic errors like the murder of the Duc d'Enghien. The first half of the film shows this Napoleon in action in the realm of politics, a Napoleon who is petulant and temperamental. The second half of the film shows Napoleon back on the battlefield, where he still retains his self-control and genius.

Austerlitz, despite its all-star cast (or perhaps because of it— Pierre Mondy's Napoleon, for example, is far less convincing than Albert Dieudonné's), despite its effective use of color and Cinema-Scope, and despite its careful rendition of the battle scenes, is a disappointing film. It is infinitely more conventional than the silent *Napoléon* of 1927. Moreover, it is not unified; many of the intrigues of the first part are left hanging. The film is perilously near to becoming yet another war film, and a paean to military genius. It is excessively long and sometimes trite. Was Gance trying to guarantee himself the chance to make more films by trying to make this one commercially successful?

In 1971 Gance released yet another sound version of *Napoléon—Bonaparte et la Révolution.* This new version of the original silent *Napoléon* extends the scope of the narrative to include the first few battles of the Italian campaign, but it cuts out all material prior to 1792 and eliminates the marvelous triptychs of the 1927 version. Naturally, those who have seen the silent version will find it difficult to resign themselves to the sacrifice of two hours of material, even if sound has now been added. Perhaps even more important than the cutting of material to make it possible to distribute the film commercially is the change in perspective and emphasis.

The title itself is revealing. *Napoléon* was primarily about Napoleon, whereas *Bonaparte et la Révolution* stresses the idea that Napoleon was the logical culmination of the Revolution. To this effect, Gance has added material, especially speeches, to bolster his historical argument that Bonaparte's real intention was the creation of the Universal Republic. In this attempt, the focus of the film has changed from subjective to objective, from the story of Napoleon through the Revolution into a documentary about Bonaparte *and* the Revolution. The essentially documentary quality is accentuated by the use of a narrator, and Gance's personal appearance at the beginning, explaining how the film was made. In addition, many stills are intercalated (largely when new speeches or dialogue have been inserted); but the effect adds to the documentary quality. It seems to us that this change in perspective decreases the power of the film.

The genius of the silent version of the film was in fact its development of a technique which could bring out the subjective aspect of things. As Jean Arroy says of the effects of the new camera: ". . . the spectator becomes the very actor of the drama. Instead of seeing an actor who plays on a scene with some kind of props, he experiences what the actor himself experiences; he sees like Bonaparte, runs when Bonaparte runs, falls when he falls. He experiences his emotions, feels his reflexes, sees things with joy, anger, confusion, or serenity as Bonaparte sees them himself."[17] The film itself retains this tendency, but the subjective aspect is constantly undercut by the narrator; the original subtitles posed no such obstacle. The narration confuses our point of view and also tends to disturb the quintessential visual rhythm of the film. The use of cuts of stills and prints also produces a rather jerky effect at times. Technical problems reinforce the difficulty: the print and sound are of varying quality since they date from 1927 to 1971. More important, however, is the incongruity of a basically *Romantic* film using a documentary technique, an essentially *organic* work which has become too composite. Two examples can be given.

By eliminating the scenes at Brienne, the latest version obscures that journey which we made with Napoleon in the silent film. The sense of the demonic, of anticipation, of destiny is lost. That lesson on islands from Brienne is gone, and with it that sense of fate marking Napoleon's career from beginning to end. Gone, too, is Napoleon's nascent awareness, that mystical foreboding of the fate that awaits him. All the madness and genius of the film was therein epitomized. When Abel Gance first made the "Marseillaise" scene and required his amateur *sansculottes* to sing the "Marseillaise" twelve times, they *became* the men of 1792. This transformation emerges much more convincingly from the 1927 version than from that of 1971.

We must share the opinion of Henry Chapier, who wrote in *Combat* on May 13, 1971: "Whether we like it or not, *Bonaparte and the Revolution* gives the impression of a flattening of what has fascinated cinema lovers for half a century—to wit, the genius of the shots, the lyricism of the writing, the incomparable breadth of the epic." To be sure, the use of sound at times adds much to the film. But sometimes, as in the tempest scene, there are silences that can never be filled by sound.

The energy and dynamism that fueled the early genius of Abel Gance is noticeably dissipated in *Bonaparte and the Revolution.* Certainly, the best sequences of the film are those that have been retained from the 1927 version. When we encounter the Corsican sequence, for example, the pace quickens, literally, and the film takes on a life of its own, pulsating with the visual cadences of the silent cinema, an obvious contrast to the slow visual bridges that have been added elsewhere to accommodate the narration. Faulty synchronization in the Corsican sequence provides only a temporary distraction, for the achievement here is *not* verbal.

On the other hand, newly shot footage of live actors seems mainly to involve crowd scenes and reaction shots, most of which are skillfully integrated. There are two scenes that have been added, one supposes, to further humanize and dramatize the plight of Louis XVI, oblivious to events around him and obsessed with his "hobby" of clocks and locks, expecting to be protected by Lafayette and by his Swiss Guards, and pathetically deluded in the belief that he can still capture the sympathy of the mob. The Louis that we see in these scenes early in the film is a reasonable facsimile of the Louis that we later see being brought before the Convention, but it is doubtful that they could be played by the same actor, for several decades have intervened. In this final remake of *Napoléon*, Gance undertakes the impossible, attempting to defeat Time itself.

The process of the 1971 version, then, is to stretch and expand the earlier version to fit a new framework and a new design. There is rather too much military "business" in the 1971 version: Part One ends with a representation of the Battle of Toulon that consumes over forty minutes of screen time; Part Two concludes the film with over thirty minutes that are devoted to Napoleon's Italian campaign. Although hardly pointless, this military spectacle is overdone, to say the least. The triptych spectacle of the last reel, of course, is absent from *Bonaparte and the Revolution,* and it was with this effect in mind that Gance originally shot the footage that he attempts to reuse to new effect in the 1971 version. Segregated and isolated in this way, the images cannot be "multiplied" to achieve Gance's original intent. What was originally an extraordinary finale is later rendered almost commonplace.

Wordsworth, in his advanced years, undertook the revision of poetry that had been composed in his younger, more ardent days; the added perspective is interesting, but the poetry is not necessarily made better. Gance's situation in general does not exactly parallel Wordsworth's: the director has unrealized projects that he could undertake with undoubted vigor, were he financially empowered to do so. The well of his inspiration has not run dry. Unfortunately, however, this third remake of *Napoléon* can best be described as a "curiosity," and though its availability may indeed help to revive interest in the original masterpiece, there is a parallel danger that some of those who have seen *Bonaparte* may delude themselves in the belief that they have seen *Napoléon*. In fact, they are two separate treatments, as distant in conception, vitality, and execution as they are in time.

6

The Artist As Hero: *Beethoven*

ABEL GANCE'S *Beethoven* takes one into the realm of romanticized biography. More precisely, however, it is *idealized* biography, whereby certain tendencies and attitudes are simplified and
crystallized into what can be intelligently treated in a feature-length
film. Gance's attitude toward the composer is summarized at the
beginning of the film:

The son of a drunken father and a servant-girl mother, Beethoven soared
from his environment to become the great liberator of music. At the crest of
his career, tragedies which might have quenched the fire in lesser men
served only to fuel his boundless genius.

In his youth, Beethoven was notorious for his ribaldry, his lusts, and his
loves. But only two passions did he remain faithful to [until] the end—his
music and his love for Juliette.

Gance is not concerned here with absolute historical or biographical
accuracy. Beethoven's love-life, for example, is conveniently simplified. Gance suggests that there were two women in Beethoven's
life—Giulietta Guicciardi (i.e. Juliette, with whom there was an
admitted affair) and Therese von Brunswick. And suggestive elements relating to those affairs are made certain in Gance's
schematized treatment, which more or less followed contemporary
biographical speculation at the time the film was made. The "immortal beloved" letter serves here as a convenient case in point, that
"three-part love letter which Stephan von Breuning accidentally
found after Beethoven's death in a secret drawer of his writing
desk."[1] Beethoven's biographers, it should be noted, have not
agreed upon when or even *to whom* this letter was written. Gance
seems to follow Schindler, the first biographer, who dates the letter
to 1806 and names Juliette as the recipient. Thayer, in contrast,
agrees with the year 1806 but claims the letter was intended for

117

Therese von Brunswick. Later writers have both agreed and dis-agreed about the dates and identities.[2] That Gance shows the letter being intended for the one woman but accepted by the other seems to effect a sort of artistic compromise on this issue.

One cannot criticize Gance, however, for not being scrupulously pedantic. In all of Gance's films the paraphrasable content is secon-dary to the visual treatment, for it is the latter that informs the whole and gives it substance. In short, there may well be a tem-peramental fidelity that is even more important than these dubious matters of fact. Rather than striving for a positivist inventory of raw facts, Gance searches for the meaning of Beethoven's life, which, for Gance, has meaning in more than an individual sense. Beethoven's music is the expression of a spirit. Just like Napoleon, Beethoven is portrayed as a kind of World Historical Individual, the Great Man in Hegelian terms, whose task it is to force material reality toward a higher expression of the spirit. Gance's Beethoven is a prisoner of material reality; he must come to terms with the exigencies of daily life, and he is not very adept at it. Gance's view of Beethoven reminds us of Baudelaire's poem "The Albatross," which concerns a bird who can barely hobble about on earth, but whose flight is majestical:

> Le Poète est semblable au prince des nuees
> Qui hante la tempête et se rit de l'archer;
> Exilé sur le sol au milieu des huées,
> Ses ailes de géant l'empêchent de marcher.

(The Poet is like the prince of the clouds/who haunts the tempest and laughs at the hunter;/exiled to the ground in a circle of jeers,/his giant wings prevent him from walking.)

The uneasy coexistence of the two Beethovens is translated into a continual tension in the film. The viewer is often irritated by melo-drama and bathos following scenes of great elevation. Even so, Gance can only be blamed for rendering too faithfully the essential paradox of the man. In the words of Romain Rolland (author of *Jean Christophe*) that Gance utilizes as a sort of *Prologue* for his film: "Beethoven would not be Beethoven if he were not *too much* of whatever he was. . . . Whoever would understand him must be able to embrace the excess of his contrasts. . . ."[3]

Gance's concern with Beethoven goes back at least two decades. One of his early films, *La Dixième Symphonie*, represents an attempt to break out of melodramatic structures. But Gance's attempt in *The Tenth Symphony* to transform and elevate the spirit of artistic creation fails because of the limitations of his dramatic framework. One of the film's protagonists, a composer deeply immersed in Beethoven's music, performs a symphony on the piano. As he does so, he *becomes* Beethoven: his symphony in effect becomes the "tenth symphony" of Beethoven, a symphony Beethoven did not survive to write. This indicates that for Gance Beethoven represents more than a man who lived from 1770 to 1827, but rather the very essence of the spirit of music.

Gance's conception of the spirit of Beethoven was surely influenced by his friend and colleague Ricciotto Canudo, author of the "Manifesto of the Seven Arts." In his *Book of Evolution: Man. Musical Psychology of Civilization* (1907), Canudo had written of Beethoven: "Human and natural rhythm found through him their absolute cadences. The aspiration to the divine made itself music."[4] Gance saw his function as *cinéaste* as an artist who paints with light, or, metaphorically, a musician who composes in light. Early in his book *Prisme* Gance states: "For new songs a new lyre is needed, said Zarathustra. Will the cinema be that new lyre with strings of light?" Later, Gance pursues the idea further: "I must give myself up to the artistic study of colored vibrations. It is the music of the future, until infra-red and ultra-violet vibrations are discovered for us. But with what money, my god, shall I make this clavier on which to play light?"[5] With these connotations of light in mind, Gance must have been moved by Canudo's words on Beethoven: "In Beethoven resides truly that effort of matter to vibrate in light, which enchanted the paradisical dream of Dante absorbed in his God; the state which the Christians call paradise." These words call up the association between the divine spirit and artistic creation that Gance visualizes in his filmed treatment. Gance's *Beethoven* becomes a visual demonstration of Canudo's theorizing and speculation about Beethoven: "In each of his harmonies, a voice of essential things was liberated, rose up, became light. *For music represents the maximum of vibrations of matter before it becomes light.*"[6]

This film was made in 1937. What is particularly interesting about the way in which it was made is that it offers a unique opportunity for the pioneering director to return to the spirit and the techniques of the silent cinema and to use sound expressionistically. *Beethoven* is a veritable symphony of images and music and for the most part the images of Abel Gance are equal to the music of Beethoven. It is not coincidental that most of the sound track employs symphonic music, for had not Canudo, who also wrote a book on *Music as the Religion of the Future*, claimed that music could give us a direct relationship with God and with all the universe,[7] and had not Canudo claimed that the purest form of music was the symphony, which had liberated itself from dance and poetry and had become *pure* music?

Here we have a masterful artist of the silent cinema making a film about an artist whose art depends upon sound and whose life is destined to end in deafness. What goes through the emotionally charged mind of the sensitive artist subjected to such a crisis? Gance attempts to show us a visualization of this crisis in an extended montage sequence that is as impressive as anything that has yet been captured on film, its artistic impact being matched only rarely by such outstanding work as the "Odessa Steps" sequence in *Potemkin*.

We first see Beethoven in the mill at Heiligenstadt and we hear what he hears—the distorted and warped sound of bells (which calls to mind the torment of the bells of St. Stephen's Cathedral that announced Juliette's wedding in the previous sequence). Beethoven's companion, a boy (Theo), hears nothing, and when the camera cuts to Theo in close-up, we, too, hear nothing. The scene is introduced by a title placing it at the Heiligenstadt mill. The following shot analysis has been compiled from a deteriorating 16 mm. print of the film, the only one available in this country, to our knowledge (though, as of this writing Images plans to distribute an improved 16mm. version):

TITLE: *One morning at his refuge in the Heiligenstadt mill, Beethoven suffered the greatest tragedy of his life.*

1. Long shot of Beethoven inside the mill putting on his coat. In the background through the window the blades of the wind-driven wheel can be seen passing by as the wheel turns. The camera moves in slightly as Beethoven takes off his coat and shakes his head in puzzlement. The boy is also in the room.
   BEETHOVEN: *What is that noise?*
2. Close shot of boy asking: *What noise?*
3. Two-shot. BEETHOVEN: *Why, that clamor! Don't you hear it?* Camera moves in further.
4. Cut to close reaction shot of boy.

5. Cut to two-shot. The two figures are separated by the window, now centered in the frame. Camera pans right to center Beethoven in frame. The warped sound is heard only when Beethoven is in the frame.
6. Cut to medium shot of boy, who turns to one side and bends over.
7. Cut to medium shot of Beethoven, his hands covering his ears, as if to shut out the noise. Camera moves in.
8. Extreme close-up (ECU) of Beethoven, hands to head, his face in shadow.
9. Cut back to previous medium shot of Beethoven.
10. Medium shot of boy.
11. Medium shot of Beethoven as he pats temple with his right hand.
12. Close-up of boy, as he blinks his eyes.
13. Medium shot of Beethoven, as he taps a bottle with his hand.
14. ECU of Beethoven's face: *What's the matter? What's the matter? I don't understand. I don't hear anything.*
15. Medium reaction shot of boy.
16. Beethoven in medium shot, putting on his coat. The turning mill wheel, which seems to represent Fatality, dominates the lower right portion of the frame. Beethoven moves away from the camera toward the door, by which the boy is standing. Camera pans left as Beethoven leaps to the piano, sits, and pounds the keys with both fists. He opens the piano, then turns around in his seat, puzzled. [Henceforth sound disappears whenever Beethoven is in the frame.]
17. Close-up reaction shot of boy.
18. Boy approaches Beethoven (still seated) from behind in two shot.
BEETHOVEN: *Do you hear? Rap harder! What do you hear? What do you say?*
BOY: *I say, I hear the piano, I hear the piano.*
Beethoven shakes his head, not understanding.
19. Boy takes chalk and reaches for slate.
20. Close-up of boy's hand as he writes: "I hear the piano."
21. Two-shot. Hand on forehead, Beethoven shakes his head, stands up, and moves toward camera, blocking view of boy. He walks out of frame left, leaving boy seated in frame.
22. Long shot of Beethoven coming through door of mill.
23. Establishing long shot of mill, sky above, terrain below, as Beethoven moves away from the building.
24. Long shot of boy leaving door.
25. Medium shot of Beethoven silhouetted against sky, hand posed overhead. He grasps his head.
26. Shot of tree branches. Superimposed title: *The Voice of his beloved,*
The voice of his woods,
The song of the birds,
Will he never hear again!

27. Long shot of woods, the camera booming down to a height about six feet from ground until Beethoven's head appears (lower right of frame), looking upward, listening.

28. Shot of tree branch with twelve birds on it intersecting horizon.

29. Cut back to Beethoven listening (more closely).

30. Close shot of boy, watching.

31. Long shot of three haystacks. Beethoven begins to move from behind right haystack as diagonal wipe begins to open from the center of the frame.

32. The wipe reveals a violinist and two boys. Beethoven walks into the frame, his back dominating.

33. ECU of Beethoven, halo spot on his eyes.

34. Close-up of bow on violin.

35. Return to ECU of Beethoven's eyes.

36. Long shot of blacksmith working at his anvil. The blacksmith brings his hammer down three times.

37. Cut back to ECU of Beethoven's eyes.

38. Cut to shot of hammer on anvil with slight zoom to emphasize glowing metal.

39. One-frame flash to suggest the blow of the hammer against the heated metal.

40. Cut back to shot of hammer and anvil.

41. ECU of Beethoven's face.

42. Four-shot, Beethoven, violinist, and children. Beethoven's back is to the children as he moves to frame left.

43. Cut to shot of mill pond, with the mill wheel splashing in the water.

44. Medium close shot of Beethoven; foliage and sky can be seen behind him.

45. Shot of babbling brook with a little waterfall.

46. Cut back to medium close shot of Beethoven, listening. Raises head slightly.

47. Shot of silhouetted bell-tower; two bells are ringing.

48. Cut back to same close shot of Beethoven; he turns his head to his right.

49. Cut to shot of four women washing clothes by the stream, talking and laughing.

50. Medium shot of Beethoven, with boy appearing in the background.

51. Cut back to long shot of women washing clothes.

52. Cut back to two-shot of Beethoven and boy. Beethoven shakes his head, then pats the boy on the head.

53. Long shot of bridge. Beethoven walks into the frame, back to camera.

54. Medium shot of boy, who appears to be anxious. He seems to sense that Beethoven may be contemplating suicide. The boy approaches the camera, leaving the left side of the frame.

55. Long shot of Beethoven approaching the bridge and river.

56. Shot of sky.
57. ECU of Beethoven's face.
58. Close-up of Beethoven's face reflected in the water. As the water ripples, ever so slightly, the reflected face appears to be a sort of death mask.
59. Cut back to ECU of Beethoven's face. This shot is held for several seconds as the composer puts his hand to his head, thinking. The next series of shots comes in rapid succession, as if to record the thoughts, impressions, and memories that are racing through the artist's mind.
60. Shot of birds on tree branch (see Shot 28).
61. Shot of brook and waterfall (see Shot 45).
62. Shot of blacksmith at work (see Shot 36).
63. Shot of hammer and anvil (see Shot 38).
64. Subliminal one-frame flash (see Shot 39).
65. Cut back to shot of hammer and anvil.
66. Repeat one-frame flash.
67. Cut to shot of four bells tolling.
68. Cut to brief (five-frame) shot of two birds on branch.
69. Cut to shot of women washing clothes in river (see Shot 49). Holds for 13 frames.
70. Twelve-frame shot of violin and bow.
71. Return to close-up of Beethoven's face, held for several seconds to indicate the conclusion of the foregoing rapid montage sequence. His hand slowly caresses his cheek, as his memory recalls the sounds associated with the images we have seen.
72. Cut to landscape shot of tree fluttering in the wind. The camera booms down to show the horizon, and the back of Beethoven's head enters the lower center of the frame. Camera holds as Beethoven walks away from the camera toward the horizon.
    Fade out.

Throughout this sequence, whenever Beethoven is in the frame, we hear exactly what he hears—nothing. The images are quickly organized here and appear in rapid succession, establishing a distinct visual rhythm (punctuated, for example, by one-frame flashes of the blacksmith's hammer striking the hot iron on his anvil). This is then followed by a visual caesura, the camera holding on Beethoven's contemplative face. While this shot is held, Gance gives us an aural reflection of what passes through the composer's mind as he "hears" in his memory the sounds that he can no longer perceive. Thus visual montage gives way momentarily to aural montage, just as synesthesia will soon give way to synthesis as these remembered sounds are transformed into the "Pastoral Symphony" (strains of which have accompanied the visualization of his walk through the woods). And as Beethoven begins to "hear" the Pastoral Symphony, Gance shows us visual reflections of the life-force in nature, leaves quivering in the wind, a pulsating urge.

At this crucial point in the film, the director's images visualize an idea that Wordsworth expressed so well in "Tintern Abbey" (lines 88–103): "A motion and a spirit, that impels/ All thinking things, all objects of all thought,/ And rolls through all things." Like Wordsworth, Gance's Beethoven has learned "To look on nature, not as in the hour/ Of thoughtless youth" and feels "A presence that disturbs me with the joy/ Of elevated thoughts." Here one also senses what Gance's colleague Jean Epstein meant when he said the nature of film is to be theogenic.

Reaching the end of his walk, Beethoven stands by a river in a moment of existential crisis, his face reflected like a deathmask in the water. The very reflection is disturbed and rippled by the natural motion of the stream. His communion with nature at this moment gives him solace; but as the images pass before his mind and he is able to hear the sounds associated with them, he comes to the realization that he is not really deaf. A whole world of sounds still exists within him. He is therefore saved from the immediate temptation of suicide, but his problem is still not entirely solved.

Beethoven the man has survived, but Beethoven the creator has not yet asserted himself. The capacity for creation—sounds lingering in the mind—exists; a dramatized emblem of inspiration is provided in the following storm scene (that takes place some six months later), where bolts of lightning strike the very core of his genius. It begins with Beethoven in the mill. Outside, a tempest rages; inside, the composer is writing a suicide note, presumably intended for Juliette (i.e., Giulietta Guicciardi):

This is my testament. For six months I have felt the solitude of deafness. How can I live now? Alone, entirely alone! I hasten to meet death face to face. Farewell. Do not forget me in death. . . .

But the storm intrudes upon his consciousness. Lightning flashes, and Beethoven *hears* the thunder speaking to him. Rejuvenated and charged with almost demonic energy, he vows: "I'll speak with Thunder!" Then, defiantly to the storm: "I'll surpass you!" Meanwhile, the wheel motif is constantly present during this tempestuous sequence. While the storm rages, Beethoven goes to the piano and attacks it, grinning madly and shaking as he plays and as the blades of the mill turn. Once again the artist is in his element, in control of his genius and in control of the materials of his creation.

This scene in lesser hands than Gance's would be almost ludicrous as genius and what appears to be madness coincide in the act of creation. There is almost a dialectical relationship between Beethoven and the storm: the storm unleashes Beethoven's power, but thereafter the power of the artist controls that natural force. The controlling hand of the artist shapes that raw force into his musical creation. Beethoven's hands on the keyboard, Gance suggests through his images, can produce lightning and thunder.

Gance's treatment of Beethoven's genius as akin to madness has a distinctly Romantic quality—the notion of the artist incompatible with the sensibilities of bourgeois society. It should be noted, however, that this linking notion originated long before the Romantic Era. The idea of *furor poeticus*, the "possession" of the poet by the Muse, a common theme in the Renaissance, goes back to Antiquity. It was Plato who said that the greatest gifts came from madness. For the ancients, as well as for the Romantics, the poet was not just a versifier, but also a *vates*, a sage who could see through, into the inner reality of things. The materialist world view of the seventeenth century reduced the artist's role to a merely biographical one: the artist expressed his personal feelings or reflected his environment. Gance's portrayal of the artist—like his portrayal of the hero in general—is a manifesto against such a limited view of the great man. Gance attacks both bourgeois society and its constricting view of art. Gance's art exemplifies his attachment to a spiritual and hermetic *Weltgeist*.

In the two sequences just described, Gance's *Beethoven* reaches the summit of its cinematic power. One of the problems of the film, as we have suggested, is one of the problems of Beethoven himself: he was apparently a very idiosyncratic person. At his peril, Gance attempts to show this dimension of Beethoven's personality early in the film, when the composer in a fit of pique throws an egg at his servant, hitting instead his comic sidekick, Ignaz Schuppanzigh (a character based in reality, but one that Gance manipulates for theatrical and comedic purposes). Through Schuppanzigh, Gance shows us life at another level, the everyday level that Beethoven temperamentally rises above. There are perhaps too many examples of such low humor in the film, as when Schuppanzigh eats a chocolate

Harry Baur's Beethoven, with his friend Schuppanzigh.

violin—the only case, as Schuppanzigh lamely points out, where
"music feeds its creator." The gaucherie of Gance's attempts at
humor has already been noted, but in this case Gance has at least
attempted to integrate low comedy into the substance of his film.

Another aspect of Beethoven's mundane personality (in contrast
to his artistic personality) that is depicted in this film is his angry
disposition. His temper explodes, for example, after he has brooded
over the news that Juliette shall marry Count Gallenberg. He bribes
the organist at the cathedral and barricades himself in the organ loft;
and instead of a wedding march, he plays the march from the *Funeral March Sonata,* to the amazement of the wedding party. To
build dramatic and cinematic tension, Gance keeps his camera in
the cavernous nave of the cathedral while his visuals are overpow-
ered by the thundering chords of the dolorous organ. We see several different reaction shots of faces that reflect Juliette's comment,
"What strange music!" until, finally, Gance gives us a glimpse of the
scowling artist, hidden in his loft. This sequence is in close agree-

ment, however, with Thayer's characterization of Giulietta's father, who objected to his daughter's marrying a man "of character and temperament so peculiar, and afflicted with the incipient stages of an infirmity which, if not arrested and cured, must deprive him of all hope of obtaining any high and remunerative official appointment and at length compel him to abandon his career as the great pianoforte virtuoso."[8] In essence and in temperament, then, the characterizations of filmmaker and biographer are not at odds.

Such essential biographical parallels are found elsewhere as well. In the film, Juliette returns from Rome disenchanted with her husband. She tells Beethoven: "I am more jealous of your music than Therese, because your music consoles you. You will give to me alone what you give to the world." In his "conversation book" (of February 1823) Beethoven refers to such an incident (unfortunately, in broken French): "She was born Guicciardi. She was still his wife before the trip to Italy. [Arriving at Vienna,] she sought me, crying, but I scorned her." Schindler says, "Hercules at the crossways!" Beethoven responds: "And if I had wished to give my vital powers with that life, what would have remained for the nobler, the better?"[9]

Abel Gance seems to believe that Beethoven can only create pure music by becoming deaf. This idea parallels a scenario (recorded in *Prisme*) which Gance had created many years before about Homer. Homer had wanted to write epic poems while living a life of luxury; he wanted to describe things more beautiful than what he saw, or could see. Finally, he realized that the Light was jealous of his interior vision:

He goes one morning to try to wrest the secret of the Light in order to be able to definitively do without it. He clearly feels that without that knowledge his own world can be extinguished. Like Prometheus stealing fire, he wants to seize from the sun the secret of its Light, and he starts looking at it, for a long time. He stares at it for hours and finally the great Truth of *living light* is unveiled before him: his eyes are consumed. . . . When he leaves, his soul flooded with sunlight, his eyes are dead. He is blind. From that instant on, he can build his dream greater than reality. He can begin the *Iliad*.[10]

And so with Beethoven. Only after his ears have become deafened to the sounds of this world can he hear the pure sounds that become the materials for his elevated art. Gance's theory is that the human organ can become fatigued from either an excess of internal or of external sensation. An excess of outside noises can make the ear weary, but the musical imagination of the artist taxes the inner ear in a way that can also be destructive, just as too powerful a vision of light can burn out the eyes of the poet. Canudo speculates that "Bach, who became blind several hours before dying, could see the Light, to which he had given all the musical breath of his great soul."[11] Abel Gance describes this process of divine illumination in another way:

Beethoven became deaf because of excessive internal auditory tiredness, that is to say the nervous centers affected by the auditory sense became tired before the ear became tired, but the result was the same. It's the same for sight and the other senses. I stress sound as well as sight, because to my mind there is something peculiar to note; the excess of epic or overly radioactive visions in the intellect alone can produce blindness as well if not better than the positive vision of the same scenes. Thus it is with sensual tiredness reverberating on the organ after the imagination, whereas without imagination the organ is very capable of great resistances.

Since Homer, how many great visionaries have paid this strange tribute of weariness of the internal sense?[12]

Abel Gance's explanation of Beethoven's deafness closely follows the explanation given by Romain Rolland. Rolland, pondering the effects of deafness upon the composer, corresponded with a famous ear specialist, Dr. Marage, who wrote: "The cause of Beethoven's deafness . . . seems to me to have been the congestion of the inner ear and the auditory centres—a congestion due to the overworking of the organ by his furious concentration, his terrific fixity of idea, as you so well express it." This same terminology carries over to Gance's treatment, as can be seen by comparing Gance's ideas with Rolland's description:

From infancy Beethoven is absorbed in his interior vision, that eyeless vision that is at once of the whole body, and of the whole spirit. When an idea occurred to him, in the crowded street, in the course of a walk or of a conversation, he had, as he used to say, a *rapture;* he no longer belonged to himself but to the idea; he never looses his hold on it until he has made it his. Nothing will distract him from the pursuit.

And this is exactly the view of Beethoven Gance provides in his film.

Both Gance and Rolland see Beethoven's deafness as inextricably related to his destiny. Rolland points out that there is a peculiarly tragic process at work here, tending toward an end that is "tragic in a different way from everything that this glorious misfortune has suggested to our imagination and our pity: the cause of the misfortune was in Beethoven, *was* Beethoven. It was his destiny; it was himself who, like Oedipus brought about the catastrophe. It was inscribed in his nature from the beginning, as [if] it were a law of his genius."[13]

Gance also hints that there is a relationship between Beethoven's deafness and the failure of his affair with Juliette. When Juliette tells Beethoven that she is in love with Gallenberg, the composer says, "I misunderstand. Repeat the last sentence." Beethoven is crazed when he hears the wedding bells, runs off to the church, bribes the organist, and furiously plays the "Funeral March" of the *Funeral March* Sonata instead of the wedding march. Is it coincidental, then, that when Beethoven's deafness becomes fully manifest at Heiligenstadt, it is accompanied by a ringing sound like that of the church bells? Consequently, Beethoven's deafness would seem to be, at least in part, a defensive mechanism to cut off from his mind sounds and sensations which were too painful for him to handle.

In the badly fragmented print of *Beethoven* we had for analysis some sequences are missing, others are out of their proper order. Since part of the film is clearly missing, the final death montage that recalls simultaneously through parallel editing the composer's dying thoughts and a performance of his music, appears to be something of a puzzle. Even this truncated print, however, is little more than a shadow of a shadow. For last-minute production decisions eliminated key sequences from the originally released commercial version of Gance's *Beethoven*. In the final death montage, consequently, one finds two- and three-frame shots that refer to at least one earlier sequence that no longer exists. When asked about this and related problems (in July of 1974), M. Gance responded as follows:

That scene must be related to a very beautiful scene which you didn't see, which was cut by those Ostrogoths who are involved in cinema, those idiots. The first scene of *Beethoven* showed a canal of the town where Beethoven was living. One sees a man a little tired who passes and who hears cries and tears from a house whose shutters are closed. He stops; he opens the door; he sees a woman near a bed who weeps for a little dead daughter. You didn't see the scene? She sobs, she sobs. Then he communes gently in the immense sorrow of that woman who had just lost her twelve- or thirteen-year-old daughter. There is a piano in the salon. He goes to the piano and he plays [*Gance hums*] "The Pathétique." And one sees the woman. She doesn't know that it's music. But her face changes, changes, grows softer, as if she thought that her daughter rose up at the end of the music. That sorrow had made her almost a corpse herself; it now has a means of escape to the hereafter. And then she turns around and sees Beethoven, who closes the piano. She gestures "Thank you" and leaves. That was a magnificent heart-rending scene. . . . In any case Beethoven dies with the clenched fist—"let the earth weep over me"—almost cursing the heavens. His exact words. I tried to respect truth as far as possible. But that's nothing. For me it's a little detail. What's important is the totality of a great work. You make a cathedral, fine; there are always very beautiful statues and excellent stained-glass windows in that cathedral, of course, that's understood, but that comes after. You must build the cathedral.

One of the problems of writing about your films is that one rarely sees exactly what you intended.

Yes. . . . I was influenced by the sorrow of Beethoven. He is a man who suffered so much. I feel close to men who have suffered much in their lives. I understand them very well; I share their suffering. There is another very beautiful scene which you didn't see, which was taken out. Beethoven was in a sort of café with Schubert. And then he speaks with Schubert. Since Beethoven doesn't hear, Schubert writes something on his conversation book—I don't remember what. Beethoven says to him, "Let's go, then." "Where?" "To his tomb." "Whose tomb?" "The tomb of Mozart." "Yes, Mr. Beethoven." During that period, there was a machine, the kind that was used at fairs, with big notched disks. It gave a stupid, ridiculous sound, not a magnetic, but a physical sound that was really unbearable. One hears this horrible music during this beautiful scene in which they cannot make themselves understood and where they decide to go to Mozart's tomb. The scene of Mozart's tomb no longer exists. Beethoven wants to speak; Schubert wants to speak; then Beethoven says "Shhhhhh," and one hears [*Gance hums the first aria of Cherubino from the* Marriage of Figaro], as if Mozart wanted to speak with them. Schubert has tears in his eyes, and they go. Nothing else, not a word. It was staggering.

We see nothing but fragments . . .

I repeat. All that interests me in the cinema is when I give something moving. I share the distress and the sorrow of the great man who was unappreciated by his time. For me it's sorrowful to think that life passed by such men as Beethoven, Dante, Michelangelo, Mozart, and the rest, without understanding their true value. I don't pardon life for that, but I would like men to understand that they were wrong not to understand. . . . As

Nietzsche said: "The edge of wisdom is always turned against the wise man." Why? The great men have always felt the point of wisdom, maybe because they wanted to go too far on the road of sensibility, to explore too far, and life brings them back. The world is filled with vulgarity. And great men don't have the fate they deserve in life. Afterwards, they are given statues, concerts—people can't speak enough of them. But they die unhappy—the clenched fist of the dying Beethoven. That overwhelms me, and that's why I've wanted to present the lives of certain great men to show that fate wasn't just with them. Columbus, that's the same thing; he was a great man, a veritable Don Quixote, an *illuminé* who transformed everything.

One valid criticism of *Beethoven* is the film's willingness to alter the facts of Beethoven's life when they do not fit in with Gance's preconceived ideas about the fate of the tragic hero. For Gance, the tragic hero is necessarily misunderstood by his times, and consequently suffers the indignities of poverty and incomprehension. Toward the end of *Beethoven*, we see the musician in just such a condition. His publisher tells him that no one wants to buy his music, that Rossini is now the rage. At that very moment, the adulated Rossini enters and Beethoven seizes the opportunity to drink some of the publisher's beer while the latter is distracted.

This scene is not only somewhat embarrassing and gauche; it is also contrary to the facts. Throughout his lifetime, Beethoven enjoyed a great reputation. He never had difficulty in having his music performed. In his battle to keep custody of his nephew Karl he was able to count on powerful aristocratic backing. Beethoven did not suffer from a lack of money; he suffered from a kind of pathological fear of lacking money. This fear led him into such questionable practices as selling the same piece to several buyers. Gance certainly had enough material for tragedy without having to distort the facts of Beethoven's later life. Even so, despite such distortions, Gance has succeeded in creating a tragic figure of titanic dimensions. As Philippe Esnault has written, it is impossible not to be astonished by Gance's *Beethoven:* "It is a work of mimesis. Gance expresses through Beethoven a common obsession with genius; Beethoven shall be the symbol of genius. Gance sings the masterpiece to equal it: a cinéaste 'composer of films' sings Music, symbol of all art. . . . The unity of conception and of style is assured: Romanticism is its subject, Romanticism is its form. The Cinema becomes Music; Gance becomes Beethoven."[14]

In a world in which the vast majority of people are perhaps unaware of the wonders of creation and of the secret and obscure passageways of the soul, in which millions of others flock to new mystery religions which exploit and pervert the sense of emptiness in modern life, Abel Gance has known how to evoke that which cannot be seized—through art, through beauty. Through Abel Gance's eyes, we cannot see the world in our own comfortable, habitual way. Man seems capable of greater things, ennobled, and between us and the natural world, a new sense of kinship is discovered, an old friendship recovered, a unity restored.

Perhaps there are two orders of genius. There is the genius which is so blind an instrument of its capacities that it does its work without being conscious of its historical meaning. The creation of a Mozart or a Bach transcends the creator's consciousness, and perhaps that is why their work flows without struggle, only with joy. But there are also the Beethovens, the Wagners, self-conscious, aware of their role. Theirs is a life of struggle. They execute their mission in a world fraught with disbelief. In this class belongs Abel Gance. Abel Gance does not have the innocence of a Mozart; indeed, his genius lies in trying to point out to a skeptical world the heroic role of genius in modern life.

7

Gance's Return to Cinema: *Cyrano* and the "Don Quixote of the Seas"

ABEL GANCE'S total exclusion from French cinema, an exclusion which had lasted over a decade, came to a close in 1954 with the production of a commercial film, *La Tour de Nesle*. Assisted by the young Argentinian Nelly Kaplan, Gance soon regained the enthusiasm of his younger days. After the production of *Austerlitz* (1960), he turned to a subject which had interested him for years, Cyrano de Bergerac and his times. In 1963, having obtained financial backing, he made *Cyrano et d'Artagnan*. Throughout this whole period, Gance was carefully working on a massive scenario for one of his greatest projects, a film about Columbus. This project, however, never received the requisite backing.

Cyrano et d'Artagnan

Cyrano et d'Artagnan is Gance's last entirely new film. It is significant that it was made just half a century after *La Victoire de Samothrace*. The source of the film is largely theater, and Gance employs techniques more common to the stage than to the screen—like the utilization of occasional verse dialogue. It seems as if Gance's goal is a reconciliation of theater and film.

The film is also a homage to the sources of the *cinéaste*'s inspiration. Gance pays tribute to the baroque—the era in which the film takes place, which preceded the crystallization of classicism—and to the Romantics of the nineteenth century through whose prism he sees the baroque (Rostand, Hugo, Gautier, Dumas, Vigny).

In depicting the turbulent days of the reign of Louis XIII, Gance once again writes history as it should have happened, not as it did. He quotes Goethe at the beginning of the film: "In theater and poetry, there are no historical characters, properly speaking. However, when the poet wants to represent the world he has conceived, he honors certain individuals he has encountered in history by

135

the opening of the famous "double tempest" sequence,
poleon sets the Tricolor flag on the boat that will carry him
the storm.

Pictographe scene from *La Tour de Nesle* (1954), based on a Dumas story (as Herman Weinberg describes it) "about a Burgundian queen who entertained suitors during her consort's absence and afterward dispatched them."

borrowing their names to apply them to the creatures of his creation."

In his effort to capture the essence of the baroque through the romantic imagination, Gance focuses on Cyrano. For although the film has four main characters (Cyrano, d'Artagnan, Marion de Lorme, Ninon de Lenclos), there is no doubt that Cyrano is the Gancian hero of the film. Gance describes Cyrano (in the preface to his scenario) as: "A man of genius, a witty madman who did not live under conditions favorable to the recognition of his spiritual superiority and inventive powers." Cyrano was not only the bravest man of his time, but the wittiest. Gance especially stresses, however, his scientific intuitions: "In his extraordinary book, *The Other World, Voyages to the Moon and to the Sun,* he proves the stars habitable, demonstrates the instinct of plants, the language of animals, the continuity of beings which goes from the mineral to the vegetable, the vegetable to the animal, and from the animal to man. He constructs bridges over the abysses which theologians excavated for centuries." In another place, Gance writes that Cyrano, "alone of the men of his time, knew, as we, that light is living, and he studied its secrets." We see, therefore, that Gance's conception of Cyrano as thinker draws him into the pantheist philosophies so dear to Gance, described in the second chapter of this book. Gance is not alone in his high estimation of Cyrano. The great French historian Lucien Febvre described Cyrano as "one of the freest, and of all those known through their writing, the freest spirit of his time."

In this motion picture Gance also intends to make a statement about the nature of love: "Conventional logic touching the eternal problem of desire and love has produced an alternation for centuries between its masque of routine and its masque of hypocrisy. The underground observations which can be read in filigree in a part of this work are at the antipodes of this conventional logic." Gance wants a new perspective on love to emerge from this swashbuckling drama.

In the film, Marion de Lorme thinks she loves Cyrano, while Ninon de Lenclos thinks she loves d'Artagnan. The males, however, are sexually attracted to the other women of the pairs. By wearing masques to their nocturnal rendezvous, each man in effect makes love with the woman he desires.[1] On the one occasion when they do indeed make love to their ostensible partners, things do not work well. Although the women are infuriated when they discover Cyrano and d'Artagnan's ruse, each man ultimately wins the woman he wants. For Gance, this demonstrates that sexual love is stronger than sentimental love, contrary to what morality and custom say: "The heart and the senses are *frères enemis* when desire has found its accomplice, and the advantage will always remain with the prescient unknown who understands how to properly take the place of the lover." Physical love conquers sentimental love.

Never before had Gance been so successful in treating love. Eroticism has gained the upper hand in this film, at the expense of the heavy-handed romantic treatment of love in films like *Beethoven* and *Napoléon*. Moreover, there is a lightness and humor in this film which is quite new in Gance's work. One can hardly avoid the conclusion that Gance was recapitulating the experience of one of his heroes, Victor Hugo, perhaps quite consciously. Hugo, the author of such archetypically romantic plays as *Hernani* and *Marion de Lorme*, wrote a number of light, witty, irreverent plays later on in his career, collected under the title of *Le Théâtre en Liberté*. When one recalls that in one of these pieces, *La Forêt Mouillée*, Hugo has plants and animals speak, one is struck by its similarity to the film, in which Cyrano converses with birds. For both Hugo and Gance, this is more than just a poetic conceit; it is a statement of their common pantheism.

The great French actor Frédéric Lemaître, immortalized in Carné's *Children of Paradise*, revolutionized the melodrama by winking at the audience. He thereby created a distance between the actions on the stage and their real meaning. In *Cyrano*, Gance is certainly winking at the audience—but perhaps not enough. The film is somewhere between farce and realism, between lyricism and the swashbuckling epic. The film is not about the "real," but it rarely attains the surreal. The first scene indicates where the film could have gone, but never quite goes. It shows Cyrano flying in his aircraft, which is throwing out sparks all over the hillsides, terrorizing the peasants. The machine plummets to the ground, and Cyrano escapes in a sort of umbrella-cum-parachute. The enraged peasants rush to the manor house, wanting to lynch Cyrano. The Cyrano of this scene is a mysterious character, who rises above the world of the real. But as the film goes on, he tends to fall into stereotypic roles: the courageous fighter, the lover à la Rostand, etc. Gance loves both film and literature, but sometimes the literary overwhelms the cinematic, the sentimental the surreal. This is the principal weakness of the film—it does not dare enough, it does not go far enough. One is reminded of René Clair's exhortation to Gance half a century ago: "Oh, if he were willing to give up literature and put his trust in cinema!" Gance's soul has always been torn between these two loves.

One also wonders whether the relative tameness of much of the film does not come from a desire to create a commercial success so that he could find financial support for his two great projects, *Ecce Homo* and *Columbus*. Gance seems to suggest this in the introduction to the scenario: "I have tried simultaneously to reconcile the demands of today's public by calculating those of tomorrow's public, while seeking the maximum applause of our own time." Perhaps because of his bad experiences in the past with more experimental works, Gance was underestimating the capacity of today's audience.

Cyrano et d'Artagnan may not come up to the level of Gance's greatest films. Yet it certainly provides evidence that Gance was still working in new directions. If only Gance had been able to make

Columbus, which promised to be as revolutionary for our times as *Napoléon* was for the late 1920s. . . .

The Don Quixote of the Seas

Merely reading the scenario for *Christopher Columbus, the Don Quixote of the Seas* leaves one with the memory of having "seen" a great film. Columbus is certainly Gance's greatest "paroxysm" since *Napoléon.* Here intuition surely is the memory of the future, as Gance likes to say.

In 1939 plans were underway to produce *Christophe Colomb.* The sets had been designed by Henri Mahé, the costumes by Robert Baldrich. A musical score was to have been composed by Henri Verdun and Joaquin Roderigo to accompany a version of the script that Gance had prepared in collaboration with Steve Passeur. Shooting was scheduled to begin on location in Granada on June 12; but despite these preparations, Europe was in turmoil and the project was not destined to be completed as planned. Moreover, it has not been completed to this day. After the war Gance was not in a position to rearrange financial backing for the project. The director has constantly returned to the scenario and has continued working on it in his advanced years. But in those intervening years he has been unable to obtain private financial support for the projected film, nor has he been able to make the necessary arrangements to have it produced for French television, as once he had hoped to do.

In a sense, Columbus is a far more suitable subject for Abel Gance than Napoleon. Columbus is like a brother to Jean Diaz, Sisif, or Novalic. Like them, he was a visionary, whose success and failure were due to the fact that his inner world was stronger than his sense of external reality. Gance understands Columbus because he, too, resembles the great navigator. Both Gance and Columbus discovered great new lands, yet both were misunderstood in their own times. Gance has always been both a mystic and an expert technician; Columbus was both a visionary and a skilled navigator. Napoleon, on the other hand, was primarily a man of action.

Like Gance's greatest completed films, *Columbus* was intended as a romantic commentary on creative genius as well as a statement about the author himself. The assertion that Columbus's illusions were so meaningful that they brought men to a New World as surely as if they had been true is, in a sense, a fair evaluation of Abel

Gance's role in the history of cinema. Even if one rejects Gance's philosophical ideas, his intuition of the potential of the cinema cannot be denied. *Columbus* is a film that has never been made because it is still far ahead of its time and because it studies a great hero rather than flaunting some form of human degradation. In a world presently preoccupied with the Modernist ironic archetype of the antihero, Gance's heroic conception has been oddly out of fashion. But Gance has always been guided by his vision, not by mere fashion.

Columbus is depicted as a strange character, fit only for the sea. When we first meet him in 1484, we see him "looking at the sea as if in a state of hypnosis. At first, he might approximate our idea of a beardless Don Quixote, with prematurely whitened hair. He is thirty-three years old; he appears fifty! A fine noble face, bearing the stigmata of disillusion and suffering. An expression simultaneously realist and mystic, which would seem contradictory but which in his case seems prototypic." (The descriptions we have translated from M. Gance's personal copy of the scenario.) A zoom shot shows the waves break in his pupils. This strange man "dreams awake." "He doesn't see reality as it is, but as he wants it to be." Columbus, still only a poor man, will tell Queen Isabella: "There are few examples of a man who is not what he is. But before you, Majesty, I am not what I am, but what I am going to become one day, Admiral of the Ocean Seas! And it's that man who speaks to you, not a poor wretch with dishevelled hairs."

This is a man who cannot find happiness on earth. He can only bring unhappiness into the lives of women. His first wife dies because he loved the sea more than he loved her. Then after living with Beatrice Enriquez, who becomes the mother of his second son, he tells her that they must return to their former platonic relationship: he doesn't want to make her life, like that of his first wife, a new calvary. In order to be a navigator, he must save up all his physical force. (In this and later extracts from the scenario, character description and shot information on the left matches dialogue and sound effects indicated on the right.)

> It's mysterious . . . almost unexplainable . . . try to understand me . . . as if an albatross explained to you why, if he falls on the deck of a ship, he can no longer open his

He is going to take that prophetic tone which will make him misunderstood by his times and which was often turned into derision. He is already what he is going to become. He no longer speaks to Beatrice but to history, which will take a century to prove him right.

wings to take flight again. . . . Why like that bird, can I never find happiness at any place where my feet touch the earth? Why am I only happy at the level of the waves? Oh, tell me why, my little adorable Beatrice? Why does the earth make me pay with tears of blood what the sea offers me so royally? . . . On earth, I bring unhappiness to whatever surrounds me, whatever touches me, as if fatality wanted to reimburse itself by the unhappiness of the beings I love for the treasures which Providence disperses on me on the seas. . . .

The Don Quixote of the Seas who defines himself before our eyes and ears has only his grandiloquence to be at his own level. He speaks to persuade himself. He is no longer concerned about being listened to by others. The amazed Beatrice is one of them.

The opposite of flotsam thrown up on the shore, I am earthly flotsam, cast upon the ocean for fourteen years by the nations, one after another. It's only there that I discover the liquid elements for which I was born. This wandering on the seas is simultaneoulsy a terrible and a magnificent condemnation. It deprives me of terrestrial love and family joys, because I can only bring misery and disappointment there. Do you understand now why for a sailor like me marriage is treason? A treason toward that moving mistress who offers me the innumerable arms of her waves, and the kisses of her spray, and to whom I am married for eternity?

> I am only the instrument of a force
> superior to my own. Don't you feel
> it, Beatrice?

Beatrice resembles Isabella, and is jealous of Columbus's feelings for the Queen. Columbus had met Beatrice in a church just after seeing Isabella, and had thought that Beatrice was Isabella. In the end, Columbus discovers that these two women are really two sides of the same coin.

Gance makes use of his camera instructions in order to reveal the workings of Columbus's mind. For example:

Shot of Columbus, alone, seated on a wooden bed. His eyes are open. He is strangely pale, his lips move without our hearing anything. But little by little, we see the troubled design of his thoughts: enormous waves break in slow-motion. In these waves appear Felippa [his first wife], Isabella, then the monstrous head of the Dragon of Drakhar [a Viking ship in which Columbus had found a valuable map], then the two alcaldes announcing the edict against the Jews, but without the words being audible, then Diego, then Isabella and her gift of the gold ducat, a map of the world, the sea.

Music genre Boulez with distortion of plainsong.

And now the beautiful face of Isabella takes predominance and multiplies infinitely. There are 10, 20, 50 Isabellas enshrined in the gold ducats. They surge forth everywhere in the frame and fall toward the camera with a stronger and stronger sound of gold which mixes with the sound of the rough sea.

Sound of gold pieces in a cascade.

Throughout his life, Columbus meets with incomprehension, derision, and skepticism. As a result of the interest of the Queen and several of her councillors, Columbus is asked to expose his ideas before the University of Salamanca. This sequence gives Gance a marvelous opportunity to mock "in the spirit of Molière as revised by Kafka" the self-important men of learning and science who dare criticize those who see farther than they do. Gance makes the point primarily by the way in which he shoots the sequence:

Certain shots . . . in the fashion of Gus Bofa shall be taken almost *vertically, diving* down from above so that the savants, theologians, astronomers, cosmographers, mathematicians who furnish this room seem like ants, and brusquely, with the *zoom*, slightly anamorphosed in a satiric enlargement. A sort of visual game of the accordion, while Columbus will remain in the normal perspective in all the shots. This formula is to differentiate the vanity, prejudices, conceit of the examiners from the simplicity and sincerity of Columbus.

When the scholars put down their books, dust flies. In some cases, their faces are three-quarters covered by their books and maps. To illustrate their argument as to whether the earth is flat or round, Gance plans the following: "Anamorphosed images show us the earth flat, like a sea biscuit, then, suddenly, it becomes round, and then it rolls. It turns on itself, it becomes flat again. Flat, it mounts toward heaven, round, it falls toward hell. It is half-round and half-flat." In this veritable tower of Babel, there is no place for Columbus, nor, for that matter, for the rector himself, who proclaims that "One does not forget God by rethinking him in every age." But Columbus has convinced the Queen and some of the more lucid men of Spain. He shall have his money, once the war with the Moors is over. But behind the curtains, the minions of the Inquisition note every word of the debate.

In this drama where grandeur and barbarism coexist, the Inquisition plays a central role. Gance believes that Columbus was of Jewish origin. Columbus's career in Spain is intertwined with the drama of the expulsion of the Jews. When he first arrives at Huelva, the Jews have just been given a week to leave. The order has been signed not by Isabella but by Torquemada. (Gance tends to deflect the faults of the Queen onto other people, like Ferdinand.) Marchena finds Columbus fainted, almost dead, at the gate of the Monastery of the Rabida. The monks had thought that he was a Jew who had fainted on his way to the port. There are burnings of Jews every Thursday. The entire population of the city is required to attend. Columbus and Beatrice always make a point of leaving the town that day. But they forget after their first night of love. The bells of the town ring; there is the explosion of the lighted funeral pyres followed by the cries of the victims. The light of the flames plays on the inside of the room; smoke and cinders come through the window. Then the cries cease. Agents of the Inquisition come to arrest them for nonattendance at the *auto-da-fé*. But they are saved by Beatrice's revelation—she is the "cousin" (daughter) of the Grand Inquisitor himself! For Torquemada is a *converso* (a Jew converted to Catholicism). In the film, as in reality, Columbus's sailing coincides with the final expulsion of the Jews from all Spain. Gance portrays Columbus's death in the very same inn, on yet another Thursday. The *auto-da-fé* casts its lurid light over the world in which Columbus lives, loves, and dies. Gance would seem to follow Salvador de Madariaga's belief that Columbus's desire for wealth and glory was in some sense an effort to get back at Spain for what it had done to his people. For Madariaga in his biography portrays Columbus as feeling himself both Christian and Jew.

When Columbus discovers America, he hopes that the influence of the Indians will bring about a renewal of the Old World: "This is evidently an innocent world, not yet soiled by the hypocrisies and injustice of our society." If Columbus errs in calling the new lands the Indies, what is important is that "he has found on the other side of the world the first lands of a world where primitive man is good and nature paradisical." Columbus believes that he has glimpsed the Terrestrial Paradise described by Cardinal d'Ailly in his *Ymago Mundi* of 1415 during his third voyage: "The earth always covered with verdure, the flowers always in bloom, fountains of crystal, a youth and a perpetual joy where nothing is struck by decay and death. I lived an eternity of joy in several instants there near Belen."

But America is corrupted by Europe rather than Europe's being saved by America. And Columbus is brought back in chains eight years to the day after his discovery of America. This occurs through the machinations of Columbus's greatest enemy, the director of the Office of the Indies, Fonseca, and Cardinal Ximenes. Although Columbus is saved by the Queen, the rest of his life is tragic. "That's life, my friend," he anticipates Don Quixote, "with the exception that it's not worth what one sees in the theatre!"

Columbus returns to Spain on November 7, 1504, from his fourth and final voyage. He looks seventy instead of fifty-three. His boat is mutilated from terrible storms. To escape the anger of the inhabitants of the port, infuriated at the death of their relatives on the expedition, he hides in the Chapel of St. Luca. He then goes back to the inn where he and Beatrice had once lived. The innkeeper, who had once made money by exhibiting this room to tourists, has had no customers since 1496! Beatrice has been missing for twelve years. Columbus contemplates the artificial flowers she made, which seem more beautiful than real flowers. "If I had looked at these flowers nine years ago as I look at them today. . . . Well, I wouldn't have left! Hearing that Isabella is ill, he goes to find her at Granada. He sees a slab with Isabella's name in the palace. Diego, the first page of the King, recognizes his father. Then he recognizes Beatrice, old and changed, in a group of nuns. Columbus, half-crazed from illness and shock, suddenly understands: "A curtain of light has just been torn asunder. I understand that Isabella and Beatrice have been one and the same woman under two different aspects. Death, that slut, has been robbed!"

Columbus gets up, his face seems to recover its youth. He advances toward Beatrice.

No, Diego. An infinite joy overwhelms me.

Finally! . . . You! . . . You! . . . Yes. . . . After twelve years! The resurrection from the tomb is then real!

He leans in the direction of the slab as if an invisible voice were whispering in his ear. He speaks in a low voice.

Christ whispers to me: "Don't cry, I was no longer there, but now I am," and Isabella says to me, like an echo in the other ear, "Don't cry, because you find me living again."

Beatrice, however, accuses Columbus of having ruined her life.

Columbus lives in poverty because Ferdinand, influenced by Fonseca, withholds from Columbus the enormous revenues that are due him. Columbus's mind is deranged. The doctor who treated him twenty years before says of him: "This surfeit of excessive imagination at the same time poetic and sentimental could be mastered and controlled by his realism as a navigator with great effort. It has just freed itself in the form of a congestion of light. It turns in disorder in his poor head bathed in sunshine, abolishing all that is discordant and opposed. A typical example of his mythomania: Beatrice and Isabella are the same idol with two heads."

Columbus has made a list of the people he is willing to see. It includes Isabella and many other dead people: "Everything happens, even what one wants." Only the arrival of Amerigo Vespucci prevents Columbus from hanging himself. Columbus confesses that he feels himself "more and more the enraptured prisoner of an immense rainbow, where, drowned in its colors, I confound them to such a point that it sometimes happens that I don't know which of my sons is Fernando!" He asks Vespucci to read the passage of his journal of the third voyage in which he came across the Terrestrial Paradise. All we see is a blank page.

Columbus knows that his death is imminent. Above him, a carpenter and mason are banging nails to prop up the floor of the inn. Columbus believes that what he hears is his coffin being nailed together! He looks at the hourglass and says that he will die once the sand runs out. He sends Vespucci for a priest and to find Beatrice and his children. By the time Beatrice arrives, he is being confessed by a priest, who, ignoring his identity, ironizes over the grandiloquent illusions of his apparently penniless charge. Columbus wonders whether he will rediscover in heaven the Terrestrial Paradise which he saw on his third voyage. As he dies, the scenes of his discovery of America flash by, metamorphosed. He sees Beatrice, and it is over. Meanwhile, church bells ring, announcing the *auto-da-fé*. Diego tells the King of the death of his father; Ferdinand promises to visit Columbus's body before the burnings, but Fonseca warns the Grand Inquisitor, who dissuades the King: "To open by fire the gates of death is far more important for these fanatics than to kneel before the man who opened the gates of life of a New World for them!" And like the scene of the Thursday following Columbus and Beatrice's first night of love, the room in the inn is filled with the cries of the victims and the chorus of the inquisitors. Then, a silence, the first silence of the work, to be broken by a chilling laugh in the acid voice of a mocking parrot, one of those brought back by Columbus from America: "Grrrand Admirrral! . . . Vice-Goverrrnorrr! . . ." Perhaps the extraordinary effect of this last sequence is better represented by the script itself:

> A different music begins here and extends through the entire sequence. Its rhythm and originality seem to fit the spirit of this sequence.

Columbus's Room
His hallucination is going to become transfiguration.

DISSOLVE
Close-up of Columbus in his room.
He thinks he is in his cabin at the
moment that he knows at San Sal-
vador that he is approaching land.
He calls in a low voice:

> Columbus, *in a low voice* Jeannot?
> Fantina? How can you sleep when
> we are so near the goal?
> The little light! . . . There, that
> shines!
> The Land!
> Guttierez! . . . The Land! . . . Do
> you see it?

Tech.
For this whole sequence, use a lens
like the "Wollensac" that crushes
the whites in making them, in some
fashion, dribble on the colors, which
gives a sort of supernatural irradita-
tion to the images.

The face of Columbus itself ir-
radiates on an extreme close-up.

DISSOLVE

Dissolve on him, advancing under a
thousand arrows of gilded rays,
dressed in his magnificent costume
of admiral, like a glittering icon in
movement.
The image becomes more realistic
and shows us, in thirty seconds, the
spirit of the part of the sequences
which we saw, when he landed at
San Salvador, carrying in his left
arm a pretty child holding on to his
neck and in his right hand a great
gilded staff which enables him to
move forward in the water, which
goes up to his knees.

The sounds of the sea, as at the death of Félipa.

The image dissolves, same place, same motions, same child, but he is wearing the rough serge robe of the Franciscans and his staff is no longer gilded: it corresponds to the miniature of Jean de la Cosa: it's Saint Christopher! He marches toward the camera, which draws back.

The music

The wind, the chorus of sailors, the song of the Indian voices, the cries of the joy of the Indians: Eicheiricou!!! . . .

All this creates an extraordinary symphony soon dominated by the chorus of women who call him and which have resounded in his ears several times in his life.

The more the camera draws back, the bigger he becomes, the inverse of normal optical laws, and Saint Christopher Columbus, a giant, holding the Infant Jesus, arrives at the New World.

We hear his whispered voice
                    Columbus, *off*
It was necessary that this begin and that a world die so that another world could be born! . . .

We see an immense herald, sparkling of gold, announcing with emphasis:

THE HERALD OF SAN
SALVADOR
                            off
The Grand Admiral of the Ocean Sea, Governor and Viceroy of the Indies!
THE PARROTS OF SAN
SALVADOR

off

The Grrand Admirral, Vicerrrroy,
Goverrrnorrr. . . .

DISSOLVE ON
Columbus's Room
Close-up of Columbus. His ecstatic
face on which can be distinguished
the marks of a deadly sweat.
Close-up of a parrot, which repeats:

THE PARROT

The Grrrand Admirrral. . . .

Close-up:
Columbus looks up at him

COLUMBUS

Your're making fun even of my
death? . . .

Close-up of parrot

THE PARROT

Vice-Goverrrnorrr . . .

Close-up of Columbus

COLUMBUS

In short, it's not my mule, it's you
who is right not to take anything
serious in an absurd world where
the best, whatever they do, shall
always be crucified! . . .

Close-up of the sand-glass.
There are only two minutes left.

The sequence and the scenario then conclude with the following
two shots:

Slow DISSOLVE to black on which have just been written in white letters:
> The death of Christopher Columbus passed unnoticed. No contemporary
> chronicler spoke of it. Only Peter Martyr, historian of the Court, devoted
> three indifferent lines to it.

DISSOLVE to white on which appears this signature:
> ABEL GANCE.

To a large extent, Gance's portrait of Columbus follows that of
Salvador de Madariaga's biography. Gance has used many other
sources as well, however, and his version is frequently at variance
with Madariaga. At times, his interpretation is at variance with all
accounts of the navigator. Gance deviates from the sources when
their data conflicts with the ideal type Gance has formulated of the
tragic hero. Like Beethoven, Columbus must die poor, whether he
was or was not poor in fact. Columbus was in reality quite wealthy,
despite the dispute over the extent of his prerogatives, but Gance
makes him into a pauper.

In order to point a moral and adorn a tale, contrasts are sharply
drawn. Fonseca, a sometime opponent of Columbus, is made a
full-time enemy, responsible for reducing the admiral to poverty.
Fonseca is made responsible for the enslavement of the Indians,
credit for which must also go to Columbus. Gance treats the session
at the University of Salamanca in the way Washington Irving does in
his biography: Columbus is the victim of self-inflated obscurantist
clerks. Yet both Madariaga and Samuel Morison stress that Columbus's evidence was far from conclusive, that Columbus was unwill-
ing to show Toscanelli's map, out of fear that his ideas would be
stolen, and that Columbus misjudged the size of the earth's cir-
cumference. The story of Beatrice is necessarily invented because
sources are inadequate. Madariaga, like Gance, believes that Columbus was a *converso*, and that Beatrice came from a family bearing the name Torquemada, although Madariaga hesitates to say that
she was of the same family as the Grand Inquisitor.

Gance's use of historical material in this script is similar to his use
of it in *Napoléon* and *Beethoven*. Because Gance believes that history has meaning, he is not willing to allow adventitious facts to
obscure what that meaning is. Sir Philip Sidney, following the Aris-
totelian tradition, once distinguished History, the study of things as
they are, from Poetry, the study of things as they ought to be. Just as
for Dante, who explained that texts could be interpreted on four
levels, with the literal being the lowest, so for Gance the essential

meaning of things does not lie in the factual. He constantly tries to transfer to the narrative overtones of the higher levels of meaning as he sees them. And yet, Columbus emerges as a real human being. It is the Don Quixote of the Seas as seen by the Don Quixote of the Cinema. Gance understands Columbus because he understands himself.

Columbus would be a great conclusion to a great cinematic career. Even if Gance does not make the film itself, he has written a scenario. Those who know Abel Gance's work can see the printed page turn to visual images in their mind's eye.

It seems a long time since a small group of men began talking about building great cathedrals of light. They laid the foundations, but the cathedrals remain to be built. The architects and craftsmen are ready, but modern society lacks the commitment to its cathedrals that medieval society had toward its own. Abel Gance, sole survivor of those men whose fertile minds foresaw the emergence of the Seventh Art, is a standing reproach to modern society.

8

Toward the Future: The State of the Cinema

"WHEN THE FILM has exhausted its technical élan," Herbert Read has written, "it must inevitably return to the poets. For the quality of an art always depends finally on the quality of the mind directing it or producing it, and no art can survive on a purely mechanical inspiration." We hope that the foregoing chapters have demonstrated "the quality of the mind" operating behind the cinema of Abel Gance—penetrating, provocative, widely read and peculiarly synthesized, innovative, and, finally, interesting. There can be little doubt that the cinema requires—as Read goes on to say—"a new type of artist—an artist with the visual sensibility of the painter, the vision of the poet, and the time-sense of the musician."[1] A successful *cinéaste* must combine these talents, to be sure, but if the work of any great director is examined, one talent will often tend to overshadow the others: consider, for example, the visual sensibility of a Dovzhenko, the time-sense of an Eisenstein, or the poetic vision of an Abel Gance. It is precisely that visionary quality that dominates and informs Gance's best work, that explodes and transcends the melodramatic structures that threaten to confine it.

The present book has not been intended as an exercise in auteurist appreciation, though there are most certainly emblems and motifs, themes and techniques that characterize the better films of Abel Gance. We believe that Gance should be viewed as a significant artist rising out of a particular intellectual milieu, an artist influenced by other artists and thinkers who were not themselves exclusively film figures. Unlike many of those who practice his craft, Gance stands out as an original thinker as well as an original inventor and technician. His best films are executed with a sense of style and visual brilliance; yet his style almost always serves his substance. And his most significant inventions, his astonishing pyrotechnics, were devised so that he could better express his in-

153

Abel Gance on location for Magirama *(1956).*

tentions through the medium of film. If existing technology was an insufficient means to his artistic end, he found ways to improve it, and the grammar of film owes much to his inventiveness.

At the turn of the century Abel Gance was one of a small group of artists and thinkers who foresaw the potential of cinema, who wanted not only to elevate cinema to the level of art, but to make it an instrument of social change and, beyond this, to make it the very basis for the religion of the future. Could it be that the vision of these men, their clairvoyance, their insight, has been the reason for their neglect? Now, sixty years later, we are well aware that cinema, far from being the liberating and total art that it might have been, has become, in large measure, a victim of commercialism. In brief, cinema has not liberated men; society has perverted cinema.

Abel Gance stands between the past and the future. He represents the dreams and soul of the great days when cinema was not to be taken for granted but remained to be created. He is likewise the harbinger of what cinema might become. These two roles are really one. Gance created the dream, then he invented the means to actualize that dream. His failures came when his dream and his techniques outreached the sensibility and vision of the people around him. For cinema to become an instrument for changing society, society had to be willing to give free reign to the *cinéaste*.

It is time to ask where the cinema is going, what the cinema is supposed to be rather than what it is. If we are ready to pose these questions, we must go back in our minds to the time when the founders of the art of cinema began asking what cinema could be. We must go back to the world of Griffith and Eisenstein, of Clair and the young Buñuel. And we must come to terms with one of the titans of those early days who is with us still: Abel Gance. Gance himself is the epitome of what cinema might have become but never fully did. With reason, Fernand Léger has said that Gance was both a precursor and a fulfillment at the same time: we must look toward him as both a lodestar for the past and as a beacon for the future.

Unfortunately, film has today come to a *cul-de-sac*. Artists have always had to struggle in a world where action was not the brother of the dream. But painters and composers could paint and compose; and if their own times did not appreciate them, they could at least await recognition by posterity. Film is a collective art, however, and it cannot be created without great sources of wealth. For the cinema to be able to play its proper role, the arts must find a new place in society. The capitalist ethic which has dominated the West must give way to an ethic which places greater stress on the full and free development of the individual. Cinema is, finally, a social art and will not really flourish until society itself becomes more socially inclined.

The tragedy of Abel Gance is not simply a personal tragedy. Abel Gance has made great films, as Eisenstein, Buñuel, and Griffith have made great films. But great films are not simply the triumph of the human will over the chaos of unformed and resistant materials: they also represent the victory of the artist over the commercial (and sometimes the political) circumstances around him. The *cinéaste* wastes his energies in the latter combat, wherein a partial victory is the most that he can possibly expect. Some *cinéastes* can work happily within the commercial circuit because they are not artists at all; some reject it completely and thereby lose their chance to make films; a few alternate between creation and exploitation, accepting the second so that from time to time they can do the first, using up their energies in unequal combat.

If the current attitude toward poetry and art is an indication of the state of a civilization—and indeed it is—we have good reason to be alarmed. Cinema, which has the potential of projecting an alternative vision of what the world might be—thereby fulfilling its poetic function—all too often merely reflects in intensified form the violence, perversity, and illness of our times. Rather than establish an ideal in contradistinction to these horrors, it glorifies them. Cinema, and more lately television as well, thus become little more than reflections of the decadence of our times. Ironically, the media become agents in the process of our further degeneration.

Abel Gance has never been able to fit in with the purveyors of this message; he has never hidden his faith in what cinema might become. But idealism easily establishes an adversary relationship with commercialism and the profit motive. And of course power remains in the hands of the cost-accountants, not in the hands of visionary artists. Thus there will probably be no money for Abel Gance to make films, no contracts for public television. When the man dies, perhaps a few retrospectives will then be in order. It is always easier and more convenient to honor the dead than the living. But while he is still alive, Abel Gance remains a symbol of reproach to commercial corruption.

On August 5, 1972, Abel Gance wrote a long letter to the then

Minister of Culture, Jacques Duhamel, a copy of which he has given
us with his permission to translate and excerpt. In it he makes clear
that in his old age his goal was not to enjoy the advantages of a
pension, but to be given the opportunity to complete a number of
projects he had long been meditating. And yet, at the age of eighty-
four, Gance regrets that he has been for too many years neglected
by an industry he had helped to create—though perhaps not quite
to the degree that D. W. Griffith was ignored in his later years, or
Méliès, who ended his days selling toys. In that letter Gance first
assesses his contribution to French cinema and then measures this
against his potential contribution as follows:

If, after *La Roue, J'Accuse,* and the silent *Napoléon Bonaparte* of 1926,
France had given me the elbow room and the money necessary to make of
the cinema the art which it could be and which would allow it to progress
with the same rapidity as all the other branches of human activity, I would
not have been obliged for half a century to make films to feed myself. I am
speaking of *Maître du Forge, Poliche, Roman d'un Jeune Homme pauvre,
Lucrèce Borgia, La Dame aux Camélias, Louise, Jerôme Perreau, Mater
Dolorosa, La Tour de Nesle, Paradis Perdu, Le Voleur des Femmes.* . . .
Instead, the cinema has remained technically where it was at the arrival of
the train of La Ciotat of the Lumière brothers. For fifty years I have thus
lagged behind myself, pricked by the spindle of necessity, without ever
having the hope of self-achievement. My former inventions—Triple Screen
(Cinerama), Perspective Sound (Stereophonia), Polyvision, Pictoscope,
Magirama, etc., and of all those which sleep in my drawers, latent (the
virtual image in relief, without a screen for the utilization of infra-sonics and
ultra-sonics, etc.)—these, alas, remain . . . unknown. Yet through their
rational commercial use, we could be at the unison of nuclear discoveries.

Gance goes on later to observe that at the age of eighty-four
Sophocles wrote *Oedipus at Colonus* and Ingres painted the
"Turkish Bath," leading up to a long visionary passage evaluating
the State of the Cinema and the hope for its future:

*Certainly, the cinema is not an Art, or, more specifically, it is not yet one;
but it carries in it the potential to become one and soon shall reign as master
over all the screens of the world. In its turn, Television, which now as-
phyxiates it, shall become its vassal. For the time being it is still Pantagruel
in the cradle. But tomorrow, escorted by engineers, physicists, opticians,
inventors, it shall meet the great creators, the modern Homers, Aeschyluses,
Dantes, Shakespeares, and Wagners, and brusquely it shall align itself with
the other arts "at its advantage," as they say in tennis. Until that time, it is*

still waiting there, blind and deaf, watching the workers leave La Ciotat (as in the Lumière brothers' famous film). We have never dreamt of utilizing the enormous technical progress which it may reveal to us. That's why the public is disenchanted and deserts the cinema.

Where is the exalting time of the years 1913 and 1914, when, with Canudo, Léger, Delaunay, Chagall (but does he remember?) we dreamed of constructing the cathedrals of the Seventh Art so that the cinema could become the Music of Light? We were all on our knees around its cradle. For us, it was the greatest miracle of the century. We trembled because we sensed that the future lay in its hands. Its fairy ring permitted cinema to project through visual waves not only that which existed in heaven, but all that could never have been seen or thought.

Alas! The shop-keepers were spying. Thousands of ersatz Lourdes and Lisieux were constructed and the miracles of the cinema put up at auction! That was the end of us! I drank Cinema to the lees and thousands of artists, like me, have been bound in chains by its prostitution for forty years! It dies of it! I barely escaped!

Today, it only breathes in the theatres in which the number of seats has been decreased so as not to show that they are empty. (I don't speak of the art and experimental theatres, which shall survive as necessary laboratories.) Nothing shall remain of the thousands of films, of the billions of feet of stock, from the origins of cinema until today; no production shall survive, neither mine nor others. I don't share the opinion of Ferdinand Céline who wrote in 1938: "Don't spit on your work, as they say. A hundred years from now more will remain of your cinema than of my big funereal drum. You have affected souls which I shall never touch."

Well, Céline was wrong! Nothing will remain of me; and if, by chance, my pictures shall be rediscovered (excepting, perhaps, the double tempest scene of the Convention in Polyvision), they, in their poor two-dimensional garments shall have no more interest in a quarter of a century than the rupestral cave paintings of the second order, whose naïveté makes us smile.

And here, now, is what my memory of the future tells me: In less than a quarter of a century, all that we were not able to do shall be done. Cinema, freed from commercial prostitution, shall perhaps take another name at its resurrection. An art as magnificent but doubtless more powerful and effective than the book, the press, the theatre, will keep television under its thumb. It shall become the great magic art of the alchemists, what it should never have ceased being: Spell-binding, capable of bringing to the spectators in each fraction of a second that unknown sensation of the ubiquity of a fourth dimension, suppressing space and time, as only several rare poets like Hölderlin, Rimbaud, Lautréamont, Gérard de Nerval, André Breton, Ezra Pound, and several rare painters of modern canvasses (producing works like Guernica, *for example) who have by flashes of inspiration given us the premonitory signs.*

We await the era of the overwhelming Polyvision of Ordinaramas, virtual images, without the support of screens; in stadiums, 50,000 enraptured victims shall see the grand epics of all the continents projected in space, the ecumenicism of religions which alone can lower the frontiers between peoples, with the new canons of new thaumaturgists and mythologists. This prismatic art, in which thousands of spectators shall perceive visual waves corresponding to their mentality, this incantatory, theurgic art, capable of bringing the crowd into a trance and modifying from top to bottom its behavior, this art is there, latent. It is in our reach, waiting till the eyes of a Minister of Scientific Research be brusquely opened, until he realizes that of the thousands of savants who ceaselessly employ cinema like a robot to aid them in their research, none of them understands that cinema is still in its embryonic stage, that it is at least as perfectible as the other branches of science. It was forgotten on the planning level while the Concorde was being constructed! Between the present cinema and Magirama, which I foresee, there is proportionately as much difference!

We urgently require scientists, opticians, laboratories, computers to re-solve by stupefying visual syntheses millenary equations, posed by the ideological conflicts of social laws and religions which up to now have proved insoluble.

I see them, these new Bibles of the future happiness of new times, emerg-ing from my memory of the future onto international screens before even politicians and writers can find an acceptable way to explain them. When things are so beautiful, don't you see that they are true? Tears of joy flow in my heart.

Yes, Monsieur le Ministre, if you want France to possess the most magnificent instrument of propaganda and the first peaceful bomb of the universe, help us to replace the old, tired heart of cinema with a new heart. There will be no rejection of the transplant, I guarantee you. And this aesthetic surgery is your domain.

These thoughts are the product of a visionary imagination, and we suspect that later generations will remember Gance as much for his vision of what the cinema may become as for his inventiveness and technological advancements. At present, he certainly may be consid-ered the Father of Cinerama. Significantly, when Cinerama opened its own theater in Paris in 1962, the remodeled Empire Theater was renamed the Empire–Abel Gance.[2] But that is in France.

Until recently, the American audience has not experienced Gance's films. The greatest injustice that can be done to a serious artist is to ignore him. If he happens to be a great artist, as we believe Gance most certainly is, our loss is greater than his. It is our

hope, therefore, that this book will serve to create a renewed interest in this artist's work and in the question raised by his entire
career: Has the cinema even begun to realize its full potential?
When significant numbers of filmgoers raise this question, then the
time will not be far distant when work can resume on the construction of those magnificent cathedrals of light. *That,* finally, will be the
vindication of Abel Gance.

9

Gance on Gance:
Film As Incantation

ABEL GANCE lives with his wife in a small two-bedroom apartment in the middle-class XVIth *arrondissement* of Paris. From the façade of the high-rise, one would never imagine that one of its apartments houses one of the great artists of the twentieth century. The apartment is filled with photos; its bookcases and drawers are stuffed with memorabilia and scenarios—many for films Gance was never able to make. Abel Gance himself hardly looks his age. Though eighty-four years old at the time of this interview, he retains the magnetism which dazed his associates and co-workers when he made *La Roue* and *Napoléon*. His voice is still rich and resonant; when he speaks, he seems to speak poetry.

PARIS, 25 July 1973
ABEL GANCE: You're installing microphones at my house! There is an Arab proverb which says: "You are the master of the word you have not said. The word you have said is your master." That's why I don't like to speak, because I notice that when one listens to what one has said two or three years ago, one wonders: "Did I really say that? How can that be?" I don't like that feeling. I must say that I've never had the experience of being in contradiction with myself. Because I've had the opportunity for self-fulfillment, without any preoccupation other than living—of being able to live. Consequently, when I have prostituted myself in my craft, alas, I could not do otherwise. But I don't think that my basic point of view has changed much since the age of nineteen. My mind was a little bit like that of Edgar Poe or Rimbaud at that age (all allowance being made, of course), for poetry surrounded me with her gilded wings. She has not left me because without poetry there is no existence for me. Poetry is the inexplicable fragrance of a flower. Braque has put it very well: "All that counts in art is that which cannot be ex-

161

lthough he has disowned the released version of La Fin du
*Monde (1930), Gance still takes credit for "certain scenes of
mic" that survived the producer's tampering*

plained." That's fundamental. The understanding has nothing to do with it: it comes, it states, it looks, it draws lessons; but, for all that, it doesn't have the fragrance of a rose.

I began, you know, as a neophyte, fully believing that we were going to build new cathedrals with Canudo, Léger, Chagall, Delaunay. There were several other friends—Roboul, one young man by the name of Kaplan, who is now dead. (Elie Faure was also one of my great friends.) A veritable universe seemed to open itself up to us. And the manifesto of the new art, of the Seventh Art, which Canudo wrote, and *Montjoie*—these were exactly our bible at the outset. What has it become? For us, the cinema was a total ideographic language for all the peoples of the world, not a spoken language, but a language of images. Contrary to what Racine says— that what one hears is better than what one sees—I find the opposite true. What one sees is much more effective than what one hears. We were all imbued with the value of that new language. And that's why in the first films I made I began searching for the first letters of a new alphabet. It wasn't easy, however, because everything had to be created. *Everything!* The lighting, the personnel, everything. Everything had to be done. I became very competent in the craft because I served my apprenticeship in the cinema from the bottom up. Later, I could climb up the steps more easily than others. Unfortunately, at that time everybody was going back down. When I found myself much higher up, I said: "Are you listening to me?" No, they are not listening to me; they are way down there, generally stuck in the mud, for the cinema is defiled, diseased. It has taken the worst possible road. It's too bad: I'm too old now to be of much help in towing that great marvelous boat—the cinema—from the perilous place where it's now stranded.

I receive enormous numbers of letters from different countries, from people I don't even know. How they know me, I have no idea. To tell the truth, I've done nothing important in the cinema except if you will, *La Roue, J'Accuse, Napoléon, Beethoven,* and, from a certain point of view, *Cyrano et d'Artagnan.* But outside of that, I've only prostituted myself—not to live, please understand, but in order not to die. Once one starts prostituting oneself, one gets accustomed to it: one ends up casting away all that is transcendental in one's nature. I no longer made proper use of my whole being. I used certain skills—like facility. I made *Paradise Lost [Paradis Perdu]* in three weeks. In three weeks I could direct a film which would make a fortune; but it's repugnant to me. I prefer to live poor, as I live now, almost forsaken, than to return to assembly-line work. It's too fine a craft to damage like that, at least for *me* to damage like that. If I do it, I can understand why others would do it. The commercial circuit which exists in the cinema is so rotten; there are so many sharks, so many shipworms. Do you know what shipworms are? Little insects that gnaw the hulls of ships until they make burrows; even the greatest ship ends up sinking. The cinema is full of shipworms, of people who have no idea except making money, making money. It's *la grande bouffe!*

If I could have foreseen what would happen in the cinema, I would have become a writer; but I wouldn't have done cinema. They have ruined the finest letters of our alphabet. They have defiled them: nothing really beautiful exists anymore. On television from time to time one sees by pure chance some scenery which is pretty. One might say that it's like a Manet or a Monet or a Bonnard. But its's always by chance, since life is full of fine things which we discover by chance. Just think: all that is beautiful must be sifted through those people who make their livelihood from the cinema. To please those people, and the shopkeepers who exploit them, one must shorten one's sight: no longer like *this*, but like *that*. One's forehead must always be lowered to seem like the others. *C'est fini.* There will be no more springtime in the eyes or in the hearts.

Two questions about Napoléon: At the end of the film Napoleon breaks out of the framework of the Old World and begins the conquest of Europe; but after these victories—we sense it—he shall be banished to the two islands already alluded to in the film. Did you also feel that once you had broken the framework of the "old world" of the cinema that you too would be consigned to an island, to an exile?

GANCE: I didn't make that rapprochement. I made the film because Bonaparte is a person who always passionately interested me. You'll notice I didn't say Napoleon; I said Bonaparte. He had real genius, both political and military, and truly republican ideas. He wanted to lead Europe toward a universal republic. He wrote that in his *Memoirs.* I sensed that he had a strange kind of kinship with St. Just, a much more dangerous man whose personality was less balanced than Bonaparte's. Unlike St. Just, Bonaparte could attain his ends without having to use the very violent means that were countenanced by the Revolution. But Bonaparte, in all his youth, right until the 18th of Brumaire and even sometimes afterwards, had an absolutely extraordinary prescience. Socialist authors, like the great socialist historian Tarlé, speak of him with admiration. Even Karl Marx and Engels spoke of Napoleon in terms that may astonish you. You mean you didn't know that? It's curious, but they sensed the man had republican ideas. Unfortunately, events forced him to make kingdoms in order to destroy all the feudalities of Europe. That was like replacing one casualty with another.

You ended the film before Bonaparte becomes Napoleon. Was it because you had difficulty in reconciling the Emperor Napoleon with Bonaparte, the perpetuator of the Republic?

GANCE: I didn't try in the first film because it ends with Bonaparte. But my later film *Bonaparte and the Revolution* is much clearer because it's a sound film. I used all of Bonaparte's actual words, and all the texts of the revolutionaries. You witness all the great days of the Revolution. . . . What did I do? I constructed *Bonaparte and the Revolution* using many of the silent scenes from *Napoléon*. With the words of the Revolution, the lesson of history was fantastically amplified. In fact, I'm now discussing with Kevin Brownlow the preparation of a three-hour version of my *Bonaparte and the Revolution,* because it's commercially impossible to utilize a film lasting four hours and forty minutes. I like Wagner, but I can't listen to four hours of *Die Walküre.* Beyond a certain point genius becomes unsupportable. I'm not speaking of my own; I'm speaking of Bonaparte's. Therefore, *Bonaparte and the Revolution* is the only film upon which you can judge my characterization of Bonaparte. Now the other seems a toy, that is to say, the framework which I used to make the later film. . . .

I receive many letters from young people. . . . I am very touched because I find that in young people there are unutilized forces which see their own personal goals and also their goals with respect to life. But life is closed—money, money, money!—and the frontiers are closed too. Why, you may ask, am I in the process of preparing a great work on the ecumenicism of religions? The "Divine Tragedy" which I wrote but which I could not produce is the first of seven films which ought to be done. I shall not die before having made two films—*Christopher Columbus* and my *Divine Tragedy.* But I shall do it! It's my mission. And during that time I shall attempt to have others produce in different countries films about Buddha, Mahomet, Confucius, Krishna, perhaps Luther, in order to show that all the founders of religion, all the great initiates, have always said basically the same thing. Can we not see that Buddha said the same thing as Christ and that Mahomet only restated the words of Christ? Can we not demonstrate that these ideas are like the turning of a prismatic lighthouse beacon? What I don't understand is why there should be religious wars, because all the founders of religion have taught nearly the same ideas. But the clergy have taken control of each of the religions and surrounded them with theater comedies; and since it's their life, their money, and their job, they can't abandon them. A fifteen-year-old child would understand that the problems which exist are problems of dialectic, *only* of dialectic, not fundamental problems. So this is a great project which I would like to accomplish before I die.

Does what you have just said explain why you played Christ in the film The End of the World?

GANCE: Yes, but *The End of the World* was an abortive work. The idea was very fine, very interesting, and my mind was pretty well set. Unfortunately, I fell on an uninspired producer—a little photographer who made photos at five francs the exposure—just like one of those coin-operated photomachines. This fellow, by chance, knew some rich people, and he sent me money to make the film. Consequently, he felt free to say: "this must be cut," or "that must be cut." During the day I brought up the rushes; in the evenings, together with his janitor he cut them. Thus, the film was ruined, though one sees, from time to time, fragments of what I intended. But if it's not tied together properly, it doesn't work. It's rather like the nervous system: if an arm moves but the other parts don't, it's to no avail. With no unity of purpose, the system breaks down.

I've always tried to use this magical instrument, this absolutely magical instrument. As Novalis said, "An image is an incantation: a certain spirit is called; a certain spirit appears." But the spirit *must* be called! The spirit is found *between* the images.

May we consider that scene in Napoléon *that juxtaposes the storm on the sea and the storm in the Convention? We receive the impression of the unity of the natural and social worlds. Did you emphasize that unity as a metaphor, or as a metaphysic?*

GANCE: I observed that for great ideas to be actualized, no matter how original, certain other conditions must exist. In fact, Bonaparte returned during the fall of the Girondins, when the Convention was about to dissolve. It was during that very acute political storm, one much more violent than those which we now have in Europe, that he found himself placed by the elements in a real storm which threatened to destroy all that he had in him. For me, the terrestrial storm and the political storm became one. And that's why there are so many superimpositions and juxtapositions of images while he appears. At times there are up to fifteen images, one on top of the other. Thus, you can no longer distinguish each separate image; but since you have seen some of them before, they exist like sounds in an orchestra. When you listen to an orchestra, you don't know whether it's the bassoon, or the flute, or the oboe which is playing; but you hear the ensemble. Likewise, in *Napoléon* you have a visual ensemble, and when you present that in triptych, that is to say, on three screens, your audience is absolutely overwhelmed.

So the tempest sequence foreshadows Bonaparte's destiny?

GANCE: Yes. At a time when I didn't have sound I had to find a way of showing by purely visual means that he could remain afloat during all tempests. At the same time France was boiling over, an enormous tempest was developing, and I wanted to show that France too had to stay afloat. Since he was there, and since history teaches us that he was going to keep France afloat, it was natural that he appear in that struggle. That's how I had conceived it. As I was saying to you just a short while ago when speaking of Braque, I only know the *why* of what I do afterwards. I don't understand why at the time I'm doing it. That's what I call Inspiration. Why does a poet express himself in words no other man would write? He has no idea; he can't explain it. There are many things that I too can't explain. There are some "whys" that can be explained. But there are others that cannot. There are times when I am amazed with myself—*ingénu devant moi.* One's work ought so to transcend oneself that one cannot expect to grasp its significance during one's own lifetime. That's why one dies, and that's why one's works can survive. . . .

The scenes in Polyvision were very important to me because that was where I wanted the writing of cinema to begin. When one sees scenes in Polyvision on a big screen, a kind of psychic flash of lightning takes place between the separate images, between the central image and the other images, which multiplies the force of what you see. Let me explain: if you see images from left to right, one after another, you add their force; with Polyvision, you multiply that force. As a result, you lose the critical sense. For me, a spectator who maintains his critical sense is not a spectator. I wanted the audience to come out of the theater amazed victims, completely won over, emerging from paradise to find, alas, the hell of the street. *That* is the cinema!

It's total drama, then?

GANCE: It's total drama of a kind which only the cinema, in my opinion, could give us today—if there weren't imbeciles running it.

It's difficult for us to understand the underhanded opposition to Polyvision.

GANCE: Yes, because they said, "It costs too much: it requires big theaters." Now a 2,000-seat auditorium will be converted into little theaters seating 300 or 200 or 100 people, as if they were meant for television. That's stupid. I tell you, they've ruined that admirable craft, that art; they've ruined it by incomprehensible stupidity. You don't have pupils, you can't make pupils. I could have propelled toward the cinema a whole generation of perceptive young people who would have been warmed by its incredible fire. If others could see as I do, had they but the rudiments of this alphabet, they too could transform any story into something terrific. But they don't know the alphabet. They have the cameras; they take anything, anywhere, anyhow.

It surprises me that you are here. I can't get over it. That kind of intuitive curiosity which you have is rare. It touches me very much. The French are so tired, so crippled, so defiled. Their very eyes and ears are defiled. They are only interested in Money. The French have lost their national heritage, their sense of grandeur; they only care about profits. A tree does not know that it is going to bear fruits that will be sold. A rose does not know that someone is going to prick himself trying to cut it. All that is beautiful in nature, all that is noble in man, should not be destined for the hands of shopkeepers. That's why I wrote a letter to Drouon [Maurice Drouon, the French Minister of Culture] suggesting that we must do what the Popular Republics do. In such countries the State makes the films. Unfortunately, they are overly controlled. I've been to China and Russia; I spoke for four hours with Chou En-lai. I get along well with the Chinese. They are a great people, but beyond the Great Wall they don't know what's happening. They ought to know. They wouldn't lose anything: on the contrary, they would be enriched. But through their newspapers and media they have become aware of the decrepitude of Europe, the decline in emotional voltage. They sense a danger, and perhaps they are right. Perhaps their precautions are justified. In Russia it's the same thing. But, as I said to Chou En-lai, since the States pay, they ought to provide theaters seating 20,000 people. They put 100,000 spectators in a stadium to watch people kicking a ball. They also ought to put them there to watch a great film in Polyvision on a screen twenty-five yards by thirty. And people would come! The same people as at the Olympics, as they did at Delphi, or at Athens.

So the film for you is the Epic?

GANCE: It's the Epic.

As Wagner intended?

GANCE: That's right.

Not only a drama on the screen, but. . . .

GANCE: There will always be people to do *normal* dramas. It's more difficult to make Epics. One must rise to the level of the heroes one wants to depict. Take, for example, that unknown Christopher Columbus, a marvelous personality, one of the greatest personalities I know—one of the two or three greatest. He died poor, forgotten; his name wasn't even given to America. . . . Well, because I know him very well, I said to myself, that's an injustice which I can repair. We ought to make other people aware of that man's greatness. He didn't discover America just by saying, one fine day, "I'm going to find a new country." No. And the struggles which he had to undergo in Spain and elsewhere, and the drama which was provoked when, unfortunately, he brought back gold. Above all, his was an internal, psychological drama, a moral drama, of absolutely unique gravity. I don't know of any drama by Sophocles or Shakespeare or Ibsen, or anyone else, that is as powerful as what he had to undergo. Almost no one is aware of that drama; but I know about it. One of the best authors, Salvador de Madariaga, sketches it, incompletely because it's very difficult. One must have spent fifteen years familiarizing oneself with all that has been written about Columbus. One discovers all that has been forgotten, or perhaps all that he wanted us to forget.

But what is the drama of Columbus?

GANCE: I can't tell you. But what I can tell you is that I hope to make it. . . . The fantastic drama of the navigator is nothing, in my opinion, compared with the psychological drama of Columbus which parallels it and which nobody suspects. That's what gives him that somewhat lunary, almost bronzed appearance. He wasn't exactly where people thought he was. He was there because he was a very good sailor; but he was motivated by other thoughts which beneath the surface held his heart and soul in suspense, up to and including his death. The death of Columbus is one of the most inexpressible tragedies ever. I don't understand why Shakespeare or one of his disciples never wrote a tragedy about the death of Columbus. It's fantastic! The Inquisition was burning Jews every Thursday; they were burning Jews 300 yards away from the place Columbus died, a place where he had already come before leaving on his voyage. He was probably Jewish in origin. Moreover, in his own time no one ever knew where he was born, who his parents were, and so forth. It was an unheard-of effort to find out.

Well, now, I've already enlightened you about a part of myself. There is an axiom of Hermes Trismegistus which says: "For all those who have a mission to accomplish, the corporal life prolongs itself as long as is necessary." I have two missions: therefore, despite my eighty-four years, my age doesn't exist for me. And if I didn't have a mission, I would already be a dead disciple.

Your personality and the personality of your films are one and the same?

GANCE: And what I'm telling you isn't theatrics: It's myself. Because there is a thought which is more transcendental than all the others: *"Sois Dieu ou la divinité, car Dieu n'est pas une chose faite."* ["Be God or the Divinity, because God is not an accomplished Thing."] That is to say, the religions are leaning or shall soon lean on each other and say, trembling, "My God, my God, with the march of time, how are we going to survive?" One feels them all shaking at the base, Buddhism, Islam, and Christianity. Therefore, there is a

new God in gestation, new forces which shall perhaps be the same
and perhaps be different, I don't know. God is not an accomplished
thing, but something eternal which recreates itself, which dies and
does not die, which transfigures itself in different ways, according to
generations, continents, and time. That transcendental aspect is
fundamental. But now I've told you more than I've ever told anyone.

*Thus Napoleon and Christopher Columbus are the manifestations of
a spirit?*

GANCE: Yes, that's it, yes. In Columbus there is a totally superhuman, Nietzschean side. He sees paradise. When they arrived, he
described it, and, for him, he was in paradise. He had a gift of
clothing things the way he wanted them to be. Finally, they became
that way. That's the way it is. When one sees things a certain way,
they end up being that way. But it's remarkable, that prescience he
had, a prescience of unhappiness too. In all the great creators,
whether it be Christ or Joan of Arc or Galileo, there is the tragedy of
life opposing them, or human beings against them who, one day or
another, force them down and attempt to crush their ideas and
obliterate what they have done. Galileo was right to say that the
earth turned. He was also right to say that it doesn't turn, however,
so as not to be burned; but he *was* right to say it turned, and he
proved that he was right. I can also say things contrary to what I
think if I believe that the moment has not come to say it. But I retain
my own ideas, believing that they are generally more elevated than
those which I see around me.

And now you're not going to ask me any more questions. I've
spoken to you a great deal, and the rest of your questions would only
be secondary.

Notes and References

Chapter One

1. Citations from Abel Gance, "Qu'est-ce que le cinématographe? Un sixième art," in Marcel L'Herbier, *Intelligence du Cinématographe* (Paris, 1946), pp. 91–92.
2. Kevin Brownlow, *The Parade's Gone by. . .* (New York, 1969), p. 520.
3. *Ibid.*
4. *Ibid.*, p. 522.
5. The scenario of Gance's first film, *La Digue*, appeared in *L'Écran* (April–May 1958), pp. 33–34.
6. The play exists only in a typewritten manuscript, which Monsieur Gance was kind enough to allow us to use.
7. *The Birth of Tragedy*, in *The Birth of Tragedy and the Geneology of Morals*, trans. Francis Golffing (Garden City, New York, 1956).
8. L'Herbier, p. 91.
9. *Prisme* (Paris, 1930), p. 161.
10. Published in the organization's *Bulletin*, Nos. 1–3, 26 année, 1926. The address was read at the "Section de Psychologie artistique" of the Institute's conference. The translation is the authors'.
11. As summarized by Brownlow, p. 530.

Chapter Two

1. *The Heavenly City of the Eighteenth-Century Philosophers* (New Haven, 1959), p. 5.
2. *Ibid.*, pp. 27–28.
3. Georges Sadoul, *French Film* (London, 1953), p. 11.
4. *Ibid.*, p. 22.
5. *Beethoven, His Spiritual Development* (New York, 1964), p. 17.
6. On Canudo, cf. Pasquale Sorrenti, *Ricciotto Canudo (Le Barisien), Fondatore dell'Estetica cinematografica* (Bari, 1967) and Guido Aristarco, *Storia delle teoriche de film* (Turin, 1960).
7. Fernand Divoire, "Introduction" to *L'Usine aux images* (Geneva, 1927), p. 2.
8. *Le Cinématographe vu de l'Etna* (Paris, 1926), pp. 45–47.

9. *L'Usine aux images* (Geneva, 1927), pp. 5–8.

10. *Ibid.*, p. 44.

11. *Ibid.*, pp. 34, 43, 67–69.

12. *Le Livre de L'Evolution. L'Homme (Psychologie musicale des civilisations)* (Paris, 1907), pp. 160–61.

13. Faure, *Fonction du Cinéma, de la cinéplastique à son destin social* (Paris, 1953), pp. 69, 134.

14. *Ibid.*, pp. 62–64, 84–85.

15. *Ibid.*, pp. 40, 32.

16. Marie Epstein, quoted in Pierre Leprohon, *Jean Epstein* (Paris, 1964).

17. *Le Cinématographe vu de l'Etna*, pp. 11, 18, 29, 31–32.

18. Alexandre Koyré, *Mystiques, spirituels, alchimistes du XVIe siècle allemand* (Paris, 1955), pp. 49–50, 55; cf. A. Koyré, *La Philosophie de Jacob Boehme* (Paris, 1929), p. 45.

19. *Prisme* (Paris, 1930), p. 130.

20. *Ibid.*, pp. 136, 299, 140.

21. Roger Martin du Gard, *Jean Barois*. Trans. Stuart Gilbert (Indianapolis, 1969), p. 83. This is a documentary novel in which the author attempts to report accurately the intellectual atmosphere in France surrounding the period of the Dreyfus Affair (1880 to the first decade of the twentieth century).

22. Faure, "Lamarck," in *Portraits d'Hier*, 2e année, No. 42 (1 Dec. 1910), p. 171.

23. *Prisme*, pp. 146, 64–65, 372, 262.

24. *Le Livre*, p. 309.

25. *Prisme*, pp. 145, 281, 80, 83.

26. *Le Clef de la Théosophie*, 4th ed. (Paris, 1931), p. 7.

27. *Prisme*, pp. 29, 86–88, 123.

28. Roger Lion, "Un Grand artiste français—Abel Gance," *Filma* (15–31 May 1920).

29 *Prisme*, pp. 61, 68–70, 72–74, 267.

Chapter Three

1. *Prisme* (Paris, 1930), pp. 165–66, 172–73. All later citations from the scenario of *J'Accuse* are translated from the version published in *La Cinématographie Française*, No. 17 (April 1919), 37–52.

2. Jean Epstein, *Le Cinématographe vu de l'Etna* (Paris, 1926), p. 29.

3. Translated as quoted by Roger Icart, *Abel Gance* (Toulouse, 1960), p. 43.

Chapter Four

1. *Prisme* (Paris, 1930), p. 175.

2. *En Tournant "Napoléon" avec Abel Gance* (Paris, 1927), p. 12.

3. "A Critical Essay on the Plastic Quality of Abel Gance's Film 'The Wheel,'" in *Functions of Painting* (New York, 1973), p. 22.

4. Léger, p. 20.

5. *"La Roue,"* in Comœdia, December 12, 1922.

6. *Prisme,* p. 206.

7. Abel Gance, *La Roue, scénario original arrangé par Jean Arroy* (Paris, 1930). Quotations from the film are translated from this scenario.

8. "La Confession d'Abel Gance," in André Lang, *Déplacements et Villégiatures Littéraires avec la carte de la République des lettres et suivis de la Promenade au Royaume des Images* (Paris, n.d.), p. 144.

9. *Cinema, Yesterday and Today* (New York, 1972), p. 55.

10. Lang, pp. 139–40.

11. Clair, p. 55.

12. Lang, p. 143.

Chapter Five

1. *Napoleon.* Trans. Jeffery E. Jeffery (New York, 1924), pp. 1–2.

2. *Ibid.,* p. 150.

3. *Ibid.*

4. Abel Gance, *Prisme* (Paris, 1930), p. 90.

5. Translated by the authors as quoted by Jean Arroy, *En Tournant "Napoléon" avec Abel Gance* (Paris, 1927), pp. 35–36.

6. *Memoirs of Napoleon Bonaparte.* Ed. R. W. Phipps (New York, 1891), I:4–5.

7. *The Parade's Gone By* (New York, 1969), p. 562.

8. Translated as quoted by Jean Arroy, p. 37.

9. *French Film* (London, 1953), p. 31.

10. Arroy, p. 67.

11. *Napoléon, vu par Abel Gance* (Paris, 1927), pp. 278–85, 390–96.

12. *Prisme,* pp. 287–88.

13. Arroy, p. 25. Further production details cited from pp. 38 and 46.

14. "La Beauté à travers le cinéma," *Institut Général Psychologique Bulletin,* Nos. 1–3, 26 année, 1926. Translated by the authors.

15. Départ vers la Polyvision," *Cahiers du Cinéma,* No. 41 (Dec. 1954), pp. 6–7.

16. "Les nouveaux chapitres de notre syntaxe," *Cahiers du Cinéma,* No. 27 (Oct. 1953), p. 27.

17. Arroy, pp. 48–49.

Chapter Six

1. John N. Burk, *The Life and Works of Beethoven* (New York, 1943), p. 155.

2. *Thayer's Life of Beethoven.* Ed. Elliot Forbes. 2 vols. (Princeton, 1964). For the material dealing with the question of the "immortal be-

loved," see Vol. II, pp. 1088–93. Forbes concludes, however, that the identity of the "immortal beloved" remains a mystery. Cf. Burk's *Life and Works*, pp. 160–61.

3. *Beethoven the Creator: From the Eroica to the Appassionata.* Trans. Ernest Newman (New York, 1929), I:57. The quotation continues: ". . . contrasts, that brings about his mighty equilibrium. Yes, Beethoven is capable—at any rate in his youth—of feeling joy and sorrow almost simultaneously."

4. *Le Livre de l'Evolution. L'Homme. Psychologie musicale des civilisations* (Paris, 1907).

5. *Prisme* (Paris, 1930), pp. 160, 73–74.

6. Canudo, *Le Livre*, pp. 192–93.

7. *L'Usine aux images* (Geneva, 1927), p. 70.

8. *Thayer's Life*, I:292.

9. *Ibid.*, p. 290.

10. *Prisme*, p. 78.

11. *Le Livre*, p. 204.

12. *Prisme*, pp. 70–71.

13. *Beethoven*, I:281, 279, 282.

14. Translated as quoted by Roger Icart, *Abel Gance* (Toulouse, 1960), p. 143.

Chapter Seven

1. This idea was inspired by chapter four of the *Mémoires de Charles de Batz-Castelmore, Comte d'Artagnan*, redigés par Gatien Courtilz de Sandras (Paris, 1928), in which d'Artagnan succeeds in making love with a woman he desires by passing as someone else.

Chapter Eight

1. "Towards a Film Aesthetic," in *Film: A Montage of Theories.* Ed Richard Dyer MacCann (New York, 1966), p. 169.

2. Vincent Canby, *Film 71/72* (New York, 1972), p. 277.

Selected Bibliography

Primary Sources

1. Books and Scenarios

La Fin du Monde, scénario arrangé par Joachim Renez. Paris: Cinéma-Bibliothèque Éditions Jules Tallandier, 1931. This printed scenario tells the story of Gance's ill-fated film.

J'Accuse. Ed. Léon Moussinac. Paris: Editions La Lampe merveilleuse, 1922. Scenario of the silent 1919 version of the film. A more useful and accurate plot summary that is closer to the actual released version of the film may be found, however, in *La Cinématographie Française*, No. 17 (April 1919), 37–52.

Mater Dolorosa, scénario original arrangé par Joachim Renez. Paris: Cinéma-Bibliothèque Éditions Jules Tallandier, 1932. This is the scenario for the sound version of the film.

Napoléon vu par Abel Gance. Paris: Librairie Plon, 1927. A shot and sequence description of Gance's best-known motion picture and the most detailed scenario published for any of Gance's films. Kevin Brownlow is currently preparing a much-needed English edition of the *Napoléon* scenario.

Prisme. Paris: Gallimard, Éditions de la N. R. F., 1930. *Prisme* is in fact much more than a "curious cinema book," as one reviewer called it in 1930. It is a personal journal and commonplace book that provides insight into Gance's intellectual and emotional development, showing how the ideas of the people he knew and the ideas of which he read are reflected by the prism of his imagination. At times disjointed and obscure, at times fascinating, it should be translated into English.

La Roue, scénario original arrangé par Jean Arroy. Paris: Cinéma-Bibliothèque Éditions Jules Tallandier, 1930. This scenario provides a record of the film by retelling the story.

2. Articles and Interviews

"La Beauté à travers le cinéma," *Bulletin, Institut Général Psychologique*, Nos. 1–3, 26 *année*, 1926. Paris: Au Siège de la Société, 1926. Originally written as an address to be given before the "Section de Psychologie artistique" at the 1926 conference of the Institut Général Psychologique.

"La Digue," in *L'Écran*. Gance Special Issue (April/May 1958), 33–34.
Prints scenario material for Gance's first film, made in 1911.

"Départ vers la polyvision," *Cahiers du Cinéma*, No. 41 (December 1954),
4–9. Gance describes himself as being "an inventor by necessity."
Polyvision was developed because the scope of Napoleon required it.

"Entretien avec Jacques Rivette et François Truffaut," *Cahiers du Cinéma*,
No. 42 (January 1955), 6–17. Gance is confronted by the "New Wave,"
interviewed here by Truffaut and Rivette.

"Film As Incantation: An Interview with Abel Gance," *Film Comment*, 10,
No. 2 (March/April 1974), 19–22. This interview, prepared and translated by S. Kramer and J. M. Welsh, constitutes the last chapter of this
book.

"Un grand artiste français—Abel Gance," *Filma* (15–31 May 1920), 5–15.
This early interview by Roger Lion provides a record of Gance's ideas
before *La Roue* and *Napoléon*. Stresses the need for people to learn the
"visual alphabet" of the cinema.

"The Kingdom of the Earth (*Le Royaume de la Terre*)," *Film Culture*, 3,
No. 5 (Issue 15, December 1957), 10–13; 4, No. 1 (Issue 16, January
1958), 14–16. Prepared in collaboration with Nelly Kaplan is an extract
from one of Gance's unrealized projects, planned at the time for Polyvision production.

"Les nouveaux chapitres de notre syntaxe," *Cahiers du Cinéma*, No. 27
(October 1953), 25–33. Gance dates his "idea" for construction of a
large screen by combining three cameras to 1922; the scheme was
actualized three years later for *Napléon* with the assistance of André
Debrie.

"Qu'est-ce que le cinématographe? Un sixième art," in Marcel L'Herbier,
Intelligence du cinématographe. Paris: Éditions Corrêa, 1946, 91–92.
Gance calls for a break with theater to orient cinema to a new era and to
use it as a means of creating allegory and symbol.

"Le temps de l'image éclatée," in *Abel Gance, hier et demain*. Paris-
Geneva: Éditions La Palatine, 1959. Gance's "Postscript" to Sophie
Daria's book (see below).

3. Unpublished Writings

"Christophe Colomb" Scenario. Examined for the purpose of writing this
book were extracts of particular sequences of the film that was to have
been produced in 1939. Since Gance has continued working on this
project in his later years, the whole manuscript now runs to well over a
thousand pages, collected in several volumes.

Cyrano et d'Artagnan. Typescript scenario with annotations, additions, and
alterations in Gance's hand of the film that was completed in 1963; 367
pp.

"Letter to Jacques Duhamel, French Minister of Culture," dated Paris,
August 5, 1972, 12 pp. In this unpublished letter Gance solicits aid in

completing two of his unrealized projects—"Christophe Colomb" and "Ecce Homo." It contains a description of Gance's life in retirement, and a speculation upon the future of the cinema. In answer, Gance was sent a decoration of Commander of the Legion of Honor but was offered little further encouragement and no effective assistance.

La Victoire de Samothrace. Typescript of Gance's unpublished play, written in 1913, that was kept from being produced by the advent of World War I.

Secondary Sources

1. Books

ARROY, JEAN. *En tournant "Napoléon" avec Abel Gance. Souvenirs et impressions d'un sans-culotte.* Paris: Plon/La Renaissance du Livre, [1927]. Written by one of Gance's consultants on the project, the book presents a detailed account of how the film was made.

CANUDO, RICCIOTTO. *Le Livre de L'Evolution. L'Homme. Psychologie musicale des civilisations.* Paris: Bibliothèque Internationale d'Édition. E. Sansot & Cie., 1907. Essential for an understanding of Canudo's attitude toward music, predating his embracing cinema as a new "universal language." Also influenced Gance's understanding of Beethoven.

_____. *L'Usine aux images.* Geneva: Office Centrale d'Edition, 1927. Includes the text of Canudo's "Manifesto of the Seven Arts."

DARIA, SOPHIE. *Abel Gance, hier et demain.* Paris-Geneva: Éditions La Palatine, 1959. Presents a journalistic survey of Gance's work; the director himself provided a "Postscript" for the book.

EPSTEIN, JEAN. *Le Cinématographe vu de l'Etna.* Paris: Les Écrivains Réunis, 1926. Theoretical speculation by the artist who directed the avant-garde French version of *The Fall of the House of Usher* in 1928. Especially influential for Gance was Epstein's belief that the cinema is "polytheist and theogenic" and the "most real medium of the unreal."

_____. *Écrits sur le cinéma.* 2 vols. Paris: Éditions Seghers, 1974. Volume One contains the writings of Epstein on film from 1921–47.

FAURE, ELIE. *Fonction du cinéma, de le cinéplastique à son destin social (1921–1937).* Paris: Plon, 1953. Presents a hopeful speculation about cinema as a collective art and an integrating force. Faure's ideas and theory of cinema influenced Gance during his developing years.

_____. *Napoléon.* Trans. Jeffery E. Jeffery. New York: Alfred A. Knopf, 1924. Helped to formulate Gance's conception of Napoleon and therefore influenced the presentation of character in Gance's epic biography.

ICART, ROGER. *Abel Gance.* Toulouse: Publications de l'Institut pédagogique national sous l'égide du Centre régional de Documentation pédagogique de l'Académie de Toulouse, 1960. The most substantial and serious study of the director to date in France. The approach is scholarly and presents detailed analyses of the films.

JEANNE, RENÉ, and CHARLES FORD. *Abel Gance*. Cinéma d'aujourd'hui, No. 14. Paris: Éditions Seghers, 1963. Presents a brief and sometimes sketchy account, along with some primary materials; includes a complete filmography and bibliography.

KAPLAN, NELLY. *Le Sunlight d'Austerlitz*. Paris: Plon, 1960. This book presents a day-by-day chronology of how the film was made and is amply illustrated with production shots and stills. Nelly Kaplan collaborated with Gance on the scenario of *Austerlitz*.

LEPROHON, PIERRE. *Jean Epstein*. Cinéma d'aujourd'hui, No. 28. Paris: Éditions Seghers, 1964. Presents useful biographical information about this *cinéaste* and friend of Gance.

ROLLAND, ROMAIN. *Beethoven the Creator: From the Eroica to the Appassionata*. Trans. Ernest Newman. New York: Harper & Brothers, 1929. Influenced Gance's understanding of Beethoven, particularly Rolland's explanation of the composer's deafness. Rolland's ideas can be traced through *Prisme* to Gance's film.

2. Parts of Books

ARMES, ROY. *French Film*. New York: Dutton/Studio Vista, 1970. The book, which is mainly a pictorial history, briefly treats *La Roue* and *Napoléon*, 27–31.

BARDÈCHE, MAURICE, and ROBERT BRASILLACH. *The History of Motion Pictures*. New York: Norton/MOMA, 1938. The silent *J'Accuse* is discussed, as is *La Roue*, which is characterized as "one of the monstrosities of the cinema, but an extraordinarily important monstrosity" (163–64).

BROWNLOW, KEVIN. *The Parade's Gone By. . . .* New York: Alfred A. Knopf, 1969. The book is dedicated to Gance. Chapter 46: "Abel Gance" is the most important and complete introduction to Gance's work written in English to date. This chapter presents a thorough account of the director's many innovations in cinema, particularly for the early stages of Gance's career.

CANBY, VINCENT. "Abel Gance's *Bonaparte and the Revolution*," in *Film 71/72*. Ed. David Denby. New York: Simon and Schuster, 1972, 276–80. A review of the New York Film Festival premiere of this "remarkable" production, which is "a history of the achievements of not only Napoleon and the French Revolution, but also . . . of movies and of Gance himself."

CLAIR, RENÉ. *Cinema, Yesterday and Today*. Trans. Stanley Appelbaum. New York: Dover Publications, Inc., 1972, 54–56. Contains an appreciation of *La Roue*, "the archetype of the film that is Romantic in spirit."

LANG, ANDRÉ. "La Confessions d'Abel Gance," in *Déplacements et Villégiatures Littéraires avec la carte la République des lettres et suivis de la
Promenade au Royaume des Images*. Paris: La Renaissance du Livre,
n.d. Includes early interview material on *La Roue*, 139–44.

LEJEUNE, CAROLINE ALICE. *Cinema*. London: MacPehose, 1931. Gance is
discussed in an account of French cinema, 149–58.

LENNING, ARTHUR. "The French Film: Abel Gance," in *The Silent Voice: A
Text*. Troy, New York: Walter Snyder Printer, Inc., 1969. Opening
comments concern Gance and the New York Film Festival of 1967,
followed by treatments of *Napoléon* and *La Roue* essentially the same
as those anthologized in the *Persistence of Vision* collection.

————. "*Napoléon*," and "*La Roue*," in *Persistence of Vision*. Ed. Joseph
McBride. Madison: Wisconsin Film Society Press, 1968. Treats *Napoléon*, that "most audacious of all silent films" (25–28), on the basis of
viewing a one-screen version at the New York Film Festival of 1967.
Also reviews *La Roue* (19–22), the two-and-one-half-hour version
shown at the same festival.

LEPROHON, PIERRE. *Présences contemporaines*. Paris: Éditions Debresse,
1957. Includes a valuable chapter on Gance and his achievements.

MAST, GERALD. *Film/Cinema/Movie*. New York: Harper & Row, 1977.
Chapter 4 ("Kinesis and Conviction") attacks the "double tempest"
simile in *Napoléon*, contending that Gance takes an idea worth perhaps
a fifteen-second montage of two crosscuts and extends it ineffectually
into a five-minute sequence.

O'LEARY, LIAM. *The Silent Cinema*. New York: Dutton/Studio Vista, 1965.
Mater Dolorosa and *Tenth Symphony* are discussed briefly (52), and,
later (90), *J'Accuse, La Roue*, and *Napoléon*.

ROTHA, PAUL, and RICHARD GRIFFITH. *The Film Till Now*. London:
Spring Books, 1967. Considers Gance the "*grand maître* of the French
cinema, theoretically the apotheosis of great directors, but in practice
always out-of-date with ideas," and later praises Gance for the sense of
grandeur captured in his two biographical films.

SADOUL, GEORGES. *French Film*. London: Falcon Press, 1953. Provides a
survey of the early years, describing the attitudes of the artists in
Gance's circle; later writes disparagingly of *Napoléon* and objects to the
"exasperating romanticism" of *La Roue*.

THOMSON, DAVID. "Abel Gance," in *A Biographical Dictionary of Film*.
New York: William Morrow, 1976. This sketch (198–200) is partly an
attack upon the "extravagance" of Kevin Brownlow. Contends that
Gance's technical developments are not always "related to the mean-
ings of his films" and that Gance's " 'intimate' emotional melodramas"—*La Roue* and *Beethoven*, e.g.—are his most "satisfying
works."

TYLER, PARKER. "*Napoléon*," in *Classics of the Foreign Film*. New York:

Cadillac Publishing Co., 1962. A breezy introduction ("Gance rushed
in where *ciné*-angels feared to tread") but an apparently sincere one,
with more stills to offer than text; see 26–31.

3. Periodicals

ABEL, RICHARD. "The Contribution of the French Literary Avant-Garde to
    Film Theory and Criticism (1907–1924)," *Cinema Journal*, 24 (Spring
    1975), 18–40. This essay covers the collaboration between Gance and
    Blaise Cendrars and stresses the theoretical impact of *La Roue*.

[ANON.] "France Films Her Napoleon," *New York Times*, March 4, 1928,
    Sec. IX, 6. Summarizes a review of *Napoléon*—the complete version
    screened at the Palace Theatre in Warsaw—that appeared in *Messager
    Polonais*, "a leading foreign language paper of the Polish capital."

———. "The Screen [*J'Accuse*]," *New York Times*, October 10, 1921, 16.
    This review of the version of *J'Accuse* brought to the Strand Theatre
    protests that the film has been diminished to the point it seems an
    indictment of Germany rather than an indictment of war in general.

———. "Screen—People and Plays: A French Film," *New York Times*, May
    23, 1920, Sec. VI, 2. First mention of Gance in America's foremost
    newspaper. The article points out that *J'Accuse* is not "an adaptation of
    the widely-known book of the same name which appeared early in the
    war," then goes on to digest reviews from the *London Daily Mail*, The
    Daily Telegraph, and the London *Times*; the *Times* review called
    J'Accuse "a fine and brilliantly acted drama of the screen."

ARCHER, EUGENE. "José Ferrer Portrays Cyrano Again," *New York Times*,
    September 26, 1964, 16. This negative review contends that "the plot
    rambles for well over two hours through familiar swordplay hap-
    hazardly lifted from the classics of Rostand and Dumas père." Archer
    supposes that "teaming the long-nosed poet and the roistering mus-
    keteer is merely a boxoffice conceit."

BLUMER, R. H. "The Camera as Snowball: France 1918–1927," *Cinema
    Journal*, 9 (Spring 1970), 31–39. A section of this survey of French
    silent cinema is subtitled "Gance: Metaphor and Distortion" (pp. 36–
    38). Blumer points out that in *Napoléon* "the camera itself became a
    snowball and was thrown around at the actors" (p. 37).

BROWNLOW, KEVIN. "*Bonaparte et la révolution*," *Sight and Sound*, 41
    (Winter 1971/1972), 18–19. A review of the Gance/Lelouch version.

———. " 'Napoleon'—A Personal Involvement," *Classic Film Collector*,
    August 23, 1977, 12–13. A personal recollection of Brownlow's efforts
    to collect portions of *Napoléon* and of his first meetings with the di-
    rector himself.

BYRON, STUART. "Abel Gance: Cinema's Last Romantic," *The Real Paper*,
    August 14, 1974, 26–27. This review essay covers Gance's career and
    reviews Nelly Kaplan's film *Abel Gance: Yesterday and Tomorrow*.

CRISLER, B. R. "Grace Moore Appears in the Film 'Louise' at the Little Carnegie Theatre," *New York Times*, February 3, 1940, 9. Since "the opera, being by nature an unnatural dramatic medium, and the motion picture (regardless of what you think) essentially a realistic one, the transmutation of opera into successful cinema is a problem." Crisler concludes that the film version of *Louise*, "supervised by M. Charpentier himself, is as satisfactory as any solution of the insoluble could well be."

CROWTHER, BOSLEY. "French Relic [*Jérôme Perreau*]," *New York Times*, June 1, 1944, 17. The review dismisses the film as a "barely intelligible fable about a Seventeenth-Century French wag."

L'Écran. Special Gance Issue, April/May 1958. This special issue includes scenario material from *La Digue* (33), *La Déesse* (34), and *Le Royaume de la Terre* (69–75); selections from *La Victoire de Samothrace* (35–40); selections from the shooting scripts of *La Fin du Monde* (41–47) and *Napoléon Bonaparte* (50–63). It also features a "note" from Gance ("sur la conception d'ensemble du cycle des Grands Initiés," 48) and Jean Arroy ("Les Fusillades de Toulon," 49), as well as comments by Nelly Kaplan and Sophie Daria and a filmography.

EPSTEIN, JEAN. "Mon ami Gance," *Cahiers du Cinéma*, No. 50 (August/September 1955), 59–61. A remembrance by Gance's early friend and colleague.

GILLIATT, PENELOPE. "The Current Cinema: Work of a Master," *New Yorker*, September 6, 1976, 71–75. Gilliatt contends that Gance "has been to cinema what Picasso was to painting." After giving some background information about the director, she goes on to review *Bonaparte and the Revolution*.

GRAHAM, JAMES. "Shadow Version of Napoleon's Life," *New York Times*, June 5, 1927, Sec. VII, 5. A review of the Paris opening of what "is probably the greatest film that has ever been made in France." Graham claims that the triptych screen was used "to great advantage" at the Paris Opéra.

GREENSPUN, ROGER. "Abel Gance's Movie on Napoleon," *New York Times*, October 16, 1971, 22. A review of *Bonaparte and the Revolution*.

HALL, MORDAUNT. " 'Le Serment,' a Gallic Domestic Tangle," *New York Times*, March 14, 1934, 23. This review considers the sound remake of *Mater Dolorosa* "no shining example of M. Gance's ability, either as a writer or a director."

———. "Through French Eyes," *New York Times*, February 12, 1929, 23. A lukewarm review of the version of *Napoléon* then showing at the Fifty-Fifth Street Playhouse in New York City.

KOVAL, F. "France's Greatest Director," *Films in Review*, 3 (November 1952), 436–42, 462. This article surveys Gance's career.

KRAMER, STEVEN PHILIP, and JAMES M. WELSH. "Gance's *Beethoven*,"

Sight and Sound, 45 (Spring 1976), 109–11. This essay, in expanded and emended form, constitutes chapter 6 of this book.

McCreary, Eugene C. "Louis Delluc, Film Theorist, Critic, and Prophet," *Cinema Journal*, 16 (Fall 1976), 14–35. Describes Delluc's attitude toward Gance and quotes extensively Delluc's criticism and analysis of a sequence from *La Dixième Symphonie*.

Nugent, Frank S. "Echoes of 'The Life and Loves of Beethoven,' " *New York Times*, November 22, 1937, 15. Nugent believes Gance's biography of the composer is "more a concert" than a motion picture since, in his opinion, the music too often overpowers the visuals.

————. "The Gallic Film-makers Turn Inquisitive Eyes Upon 'Lucrezia Borgia' and Her Family," *New York Times*, October 13, 1937, 27. A negative review of a film that is "two-dimensional at best, long on incident, broad on dialogue and scene, but woefully lacking in dramatic highs and lows."

————. " 'That They May Live,' a Bitter Tragedy of the War," *New York Times*, November 7, 1939, 31. This review praises the sound version of *J'Accuse*: " . . . a tortured cry for peace and the brotherhood of man, and now that the world is at war . . . the film cannot even be shown in France: its message is dangerous propaganda."

Stenhouse, Charles E. "Cinema Literature: France," *Close Up*, 7 (November 1930), 335–40. Includes comments from and about Gance's *Prisme*, Cendrars's *Anthologie Nègre*, and Jean Epstein's *Cinéma*.

Strauss, Theodore. " 'Four Flights to Love,' " *New York Times*, April 13, 1942, 12. This review describes *Paradis Perdu* as "the sort of tearful and lovelorn romance over which adolescent girls are wont to sigh."

Thompson, Howard. "Film Festival: 1927 Vintage." *New York Times*, September 25, 1967, 56. Thompson observes that the original *Napoléon*, some forty years later, "still stands as a towering example of film art." The festival audience approved of the "double-tempest" montage: "The sight of the hero's mastering a skiff in a storm, as the camera suddenly swept over a boiling, revolutionary crowd like a wave, drew solid applause."

Weinberg, Herman G. "Pionnier du cinéma," *MD* (September 1966), 242–248. A career pictorial sketch, amply illustrated, by the man Fritz Lang once called the "Boswell of the art of our century: Film."

Welsh, James M., and Steven Philip Kramer. "Abel Gance's Accusation Against War," *Cinema Journal*, 14 (Spring 1975), 55–67. This essay represents an earlier version of chapter 3 of this book.

4. Bibliographical Article

Esnault, Philippe. "Filmographie d'Abel Gance," *Cahiers du Cinéma*, No. 42 (January 1955), 18–23. A comprehensive listing done in consultation with Gance.

5. Available Films About Abel Gance

Appropriately, two good documentary films that have been made about Abel Gance are available in English. Kevin Brownlow's *The Charm of Dynamite*, the longer of the two, is now distributed by Images Motion Picture Rental Library (2 Purdy Avenue, Rye, New York 10580). Brownlow's film effectively conveys a sense of Gance's personal dynamism; it does not span his whole career, but examines his most creative "silent" period in detail, unfortunately at the expense of the later sound films. Nelly Kaplan's *Abel Gance, Yesterday and Tomorrow* (Paris: Office de documentation par le film, 1964), on the other hand, presents an admirable survey of the director's complete career and illustrates his major films with nicely tinted clips, though not so extensively on *La Roue* and *Napoléon* as Brownlow. In a voiced-over narration Abel Gance discusses the highlights of his career in Kaplan's film and details his inventions. An English version of this film, which runs to twenty-eight minutes, has been distributed by Contemporary/McGraw-Hill Films (Princeton Road, Hightstown, New Jersey 08520).

Filmography

In constructing this filmography, we have collated the lists prepared by Philippe Esnault ("Filmographie d'Abel Gance") that appeared in *Cahiers du Cinéma* and by René Jeanne and Charles Ford in their book *Abel Gance* (Cinéma d'aujourd 'hui, No. 14). We have also incorporated casting and production information from Kevin Brownlow's *The Parade's Gone By* and from contemporary reviews. The Esnault listing is by far the most comprehensive and was done in consultation with Gance himself. In addition to the titles listed below, there are two documentary treatments that deal with the making of two of Gance's most important films—*En Tournant La Roue* (1920/21) and *En Tournant Napoleon* (1925/26)—about which further information is currently unavailable. Unless otherwise noted, Gance both directed and wrote scenarios for all of the following films. United States distribution for Gance's major films will be handled by Images Motion Picture Rental Library, 2 Purdy Avenue, Rye, New York 10580.

1. Early Works for Le Film Français

LA DIGUE, OU POUR SAUVER LA HOLLANDE (1911)
Cast: Pierre Renoir, Roger Lévy, Paulette Noizeux.
Gance founded the production company.

LE NÈGRE BLANC (1912)
Cast: Abel Gance, Jean Toulout.

IL Y A DES PIEDS AU PLAFOND (1912)
Cast: Jean Toulout, Mathilde Thizeau.

LE MASQUE D' HORREUR (1912)
Cast: Edouard de Max, Jean Toulout, Charles de Rochefort.

2. Early Works For Le Film D'Art

UN DRAME AU CHÂTEAU D'ACRE [LES MORTS REVIENNENT-ILS?] (1914/15)

184

Cast: Aurèle Sydney, Jeanne Briey, Maillard, Jacques Volnys.
Made in five days, at a cost of 5,000 francs.

LA FOLIE DU DOCTEUR TUBE (1915/16)
Cinematographer: Léonce-Henry Burel (assisted by Wentzel?)
Cast: Albert Dieudonné, and others.
Running time: Two reels.

L'ENIGME DE DIX HEURES (1916)
Cinematographer: L.-H. Burel.
Cast: Aurèle Sydney, Maillard, Keppens, Doriana, Paulette Noizeux.

LE FLEUR DES RUINES (1916)
Cinematographer: L.-H. Burel.
Cast: Aurèle Sydney, Louise Colliney.

L'HÉROÏSME DE PADDY (1916)
Cinematographer: L.-H. Burel.
Cast: Albert Dieudonné, Georges Raulin, Louise Colliney.

FIORITURES [LA SOURCE DE BEAUTÉ] (1916)
Cinematographer: L.-H. Burel.
Cast: Jane Marken, Maud Richard, Léon Mathot.

LE FOU DE LA FALAISE (1916)
Cinematographers: Burel and Dubois.
Cast: Albert Dieudonné, Georges Raulin, Yvonne Sergyl, Maillard.

CE QUE LES FLOTS RACONTENT (1916)
Cinematographers: Burel and Dubois.
Cast: Albert Dieudonné, Georges Raulin, Maillard, Yvonne Sergyl.

LE PÉRISCOPE (1916)
Cinematographers: Burel and Dubois.
Cast: Albert Dieudonné, Georges Raulin, Maillard, Yvonne Sergyl.

BARBEROUSSE (1916)
Cinematographers: Burel and Dubois.
Cast: Léon Mathot, Keppens, Maillard, Doriani, Maud Richard, Jeanne
Briey.

LES GAZ MORTELS [LE BROUILLARD SUR LA VILLE] (1916)
Cinematographers: Burel and Dubois.
Cast: Léon Mathot, Keppens, Doriani, Maillard, Maud Richard.

STRASS ET COMPAGNIE (1916)
Cast: Gaston Michael, Harry Baur, Jean Yonnel.

LE DROIT À LA VIE (1917)
Cinematographer: L.-H. Burel.
Cast: Léon Mathot, Paul Vermoyal, Georges Paulais, Gildès, Andrée Brabant.

LA ZONE DE LA MORT (1917)
Cinematographer: L.-H. Burel.
Cast: Léon Mathot, Paul Vermoyal, Gaston Modot, Andrée Brabant, Georges Paulais, Gildès.

MATER DOLOROSA (1917)
Cinematographer: L.-H. Burel.
Cast: Emmy Lynn, Firmin Gémier, Armand Tallier, Gaston Modot.
Cost: 45,000 francs.

LA DIXIÉME SYMPHONIE (1918)
Cinematographer: L.-H. Burel.
Music: Michel-Maurice Lévy.
Editor: Marguerite Beaugé.
Cast: Séverin-Mars (E. Damour), Emmy Lynn (Eve Dinant), Jean Toulout (F. Ryce), Elisabeth Nizan (Claire), André Lefaur (Marquis), Arianne Hugon.
Shot in twelve days for 60,000 francs.

3. Major Silent Films

J'ACCUSE (Charles Pathé, 1918/19)
Assistant: Blaise Cendrars.
Cinematographers: Burel, Bujard, Forster.
Editor: Andrée Danis.
Cast: Séverin-Mars (François Laurin), Romuald Joubé (Jean Diaz), Marise Dauvray (Edith), Maxime Desjardins, Blaise Cendrars, Mme. Decori.
Cost: 456,000 francs.
Running time: Approximately three hours.

LA ROUE (Charles Pathé, 1920/21)
Assistant: Blaise Cendrars.
Cinematographers: Burel, Bujard, Duverger, and Brun.
Music: Arthur Honegger.
Editor: Marguerite Beaugé.
Cast: Séverin-Mars (Sisif), Ivy Close (Norma), Gabriel de Gravone (Elie),

Pierre Magnier (M. de Hersan), Georges Teroff (Machefer), Maxudian, Gil Clary.

Cost 1,250,000 francs (?).

Running time: Twelve reels (the version distributed by Pathé; Brownlow reports a complete print of thirty-two reels was once held by the Moscow Academy). The 16 mm. print advertised by Images Motion Picture Rental Library (but not available as of this writing) runs to 210 minutes. The Images print derives from the 1928 re-release of the film.

Premiere: Paris, April 1923, at the Gaumont-Palace.

AU SECOURS! (Produced by Abel Gance, 1923)
Scenario: Abel Gance and Max Linder.
Cinematographer: Specht.
Cast: Max Linder, Jean Toulout, Gina Palerme.
Running time: Three reels (?).

NAPOLÉON VU PAR ABEL GANCE (Westi [Wengoroff and Hugo Stinnes]/Société générale de films, 1925/26).
Cinematographers: Jules Kruger, Léonce-Henry Burel, Jean-Paul Mundwiller, assisted by Lucas, Briquet, Emile Pierre, and Roger Hubert.
Assistants: Henry Krauss (for acting), Wladimir Tourjansky, André Andreani, Alexandre Volkoff, Pierre Danis, Georges Lampin, Louis Osmont.
Consultants: Jean Arroy, Jean Mitry, Sacher Purnal.
Set decoration: Alexandre Benois, Schildnecht, Jacouty, Meinhardt. Lourie.
Music: Arthur Honegger.
Editors: Marguerite Beaugé and Henriette Pinson.
Cast: Albert Dieudonné (Bonaparte), Vladimir Roudenko (young Bonaparte), Edmond van Daele (Robespierre), Alexandre Koubitsky (Danton), Antonin Artaud (Marat), Abel Gance (Saint-Just), Pierre Batcheff (Hoche), Maxudian (Barras), Chakatouny (Pozzo di Borgo), Philippe Hériat (Salicetti), Nicolas Koline (Tristan Fleuri), Daniel Mendaille (Fréron), Alexandre Bernard (Dugommier), Philippe Rolla (Masséna), Robert Vidalin (Camille Desmoulins), Roger Blum (Talma), Paul Amiot (Fouquier-Tinville), Boudreau (La Fayette), Georges Lampin (Joseph Bonaparte), Alberty (J.-J. Rousseau), R. de Ansorena (Desaix), Jack Rye (Louis XVI), Armand Bernard (Jean-Jean), Albert Bras (Monge), Georges Cahuzac (Beauharnais), Favière (Fouché), Harry Krimer (Rouget de Lisle), Genica Missirio (Murat), Rauzena (Lucien Bonaparte) Viguier (Couthon), Vonelly (André Chenier), Jean d'Yd (La Bussière), Gina Manès (Joséphine de Beauharnais), Annabella (Violine Fleuri), Suzanne Blanchetti (Marie-Antoinette), Eugénie Buffet

(Letizia Banaparte), Damia (la Marseillaise), Yvette Dieudonné (Elisa
Bonaparte), Marguerite Gance (Charlotte Corday), Simone Genevois
(Pauline Bonaparte), Andrée Standard, Pierrette Lugan, Francine
Mussey, Suzy Vernon, Mlle. Carvalho, Sylvie Gance, Boris Fas-
tovitch, M. Guibert, Maupin, Blin, Bonvallet, Daniel Burret, Silvio
Gavicchia, Caillard, M. de Canolle, Chabez, Roger Chantal, M. Pérès,
Pierre Ferval.
Running time: Thirty-two reels.
Premiere: Paris Opéra, April 7, 1927.
16 mm. rental: Images Motion Picture Rental Library plans to distribute
Kevin Brownlow's "complete" reconstruction, approximately five
hours long. It will be available in 16 mm. and 35 mm. in a triple-screen
version.

MARINES and **CRISTEAUX** (1928)
Short experimental footage for the "Triple Screen," scripted and directed
by Abel Gance, and shot by the camera crew for *Napoléon*.

4. Sound Films

LA FIN DU MONDE (L'Ecran d'Art [Ivanoff], 1929/30)
Directors: Abel Gance, in conjunction with Jean Epstein, Walter
Ruttmann, Popoff, Etievant, Sauvage, and Edmond T. Greville.
Screenplay: Abel Gance, inspired by Camille Flammarion.
Cinematographers: Jules Kruger, Forster, Roger Hubert.
Set decoration: Lazare Meerson.
Editor: Mme. Bruyère.
Cast: Victor Francen, Sanson Fainsilber, Georges Colin, Jean D'Yd, Abel
Gance, Colette Darfeuil, Wanda Gréville, Monique Rolland, Sylvie
Grenade.
Sound: "Perspective Sound" invented by Abel Gance and André Debrie for
use in this film and patented August 13, 1929.

MATER DOLOROSA (S.E.D.I.F. [Arcy Film Production], 1932)
Cinematographer: Roger Hubert.
Set decoration: Robert Gys.
Editor: Andrée Danis.
Cast: Line Noro (Marthe Berliac), Gaby Triquet (Claudine), Sanson Fain-
silber (Claude Berliac), Gaston Dubosc (Jean), Jean Galland (Gilles
Berliac), Antonin Artaud (D'Hornis).
Cost: A new version in sound, shot in sixteen days on a budget of 1,050,000
francs. Released in the United States under the title *Le Serment*,
March 1934.

LE MAÎTRE DE FORGES (Fernand Rivers, 1933)
Producer: Fernand Rivers.
Screenplay: Abel Gance, adapted from the novel by Georges Ohnet.
Cinematographer: Harry Stradling.
Music: Henri Verdun.
Cast: Gaby Morlay, Jane Marken, Paul Andral, Christiane Delyne, Henri
    Rollan, Jacques Dumesnil.

POLICHE (Films Criterium, 1934)
Assistant: Henri Decoin.
Screenplay: Abel Gance, adapted from a play by Henri Bataille.
Cinematographer: Roger Hubert.
Music: Henri Verdun.
Cast: Marie Bell, Edith Mera, Violaine Barry, Betty Daussmond, Catherine
    Fontenay, Constant Rémy, Pierre Larquey, Romain Bouquet,
    Alexandre D'Arcy, Marcel Delaître, Pierre Finaly, Pierre Dac.

LA DAME AUX CAMÉLIAS (Fernand Rivers, 1934)
Producer: Fernand Rivers.
Screenplay: Abel Gance, from the original of Alexandre Dumas, fils.
Cinematographers: Harry Stradling, Roger Hubert, Jules Kruger.
Music: Reynaldo Hahn.
Cast: Yvonne Printemps, Jane Marken, Irma Génin, Andrée Lafayette,
    Pierre Fresnay, Lugné-Poë, Armand Lurville, André Dubosc, Armon-
    tel.
Cost: 2,000,000 francs.

NAPOLEON BONAPARTE (New sound version produced by Abel Gance,
    1934)
Assistants: Claude Vermorel and Robert Bossis.
Cinematographer: Briquet.
Music: Henri Verdun.
Cast (in addition to the actors of the silent version): Marcel Delaître, Ar-
    mand Lurville, José Squinquel, André Mauloy, Jane Marken, Gaby
    Triquet, Mary Lou, the younger Rivers; the voices of Sanson Fain-
    silber and Wladimir Sokoloff, and other actors of the principal scenes of
    the 1927 silent version.
Cost: 725,000 francs.

LE ROMAN D'UN JEUNE HOMME PAUVRE (Maurice Lehmann, 1935)
Producer: Maurice Lehmann.
Screenplay: Abel Gance, from the novel of the same name by Octave
    Feuillet.
Dialogue: Claude Vermorel.

Cinematographer: Roger Hubert.
Set decoration: Robert Gys.
Cast: Marie Bell, Pauline Carton, Marcelle Prince, Marthe Mellot, Pierre
    Fresnay, Saturnin Fabre, Jean Fleur, André Baugé, Marcel Delaître,
    André Dubosc, Marnay.
Cost: 1,600,000 francs.

LUCRÈCE BORGIA (La Compagnie du Cinéma/Gallic Films, 1935)
Producer: Henri Ullmann.
Screenplay: Leopold Marchand and Henri Vendresse.
Cinematographer: Roger Hubert.
Music: Marcel Lattès.
Editor: Sam Citron.
Cast: Edwige Feuillère (Lucrezia Borgia), Gabriel Gabrio (César Borgia),
    Maurice Escande (Giovanni, Duke of Gandia), Roger Karl (Pope Alex-
    ander VI), Josette Day (Sancia), Jacques Dumesnil (Sforza, Duke of
    Milan), Antonin Artaud (Savonarola), Max Michel (Alfonso of Aragon),
    Gaston Modot, Phillippe Hériat, René Bergeron, Daniel Mendaille,
    Georges Prieur, Jacques Cossin, Aimé Clariond (Machiavelli).
Running time: 80 minutes.
16 mm. rental: To be distributed by Images Motion Picture Rental Library.

UN GRANDE AMOUR DE BEETHOVEN (Générales Productions, 1936)
Assistants: Jean Arroy and Le Pelletier (?).
Dialogue: Steve Passeur.
Cinematographers: Robert Le Febvre and Marc Fossard.
Set decoration: Jacques Colombier.
Costumes: Henri Mahé.
Editor: Marguerite Beaugé.
Music: Orchestre de la Société des Concerts du Conservatoire de Paris,
    directed by Philippe Gaubert.
Musical arrangements: Louis Masson.
Cast: Harry Baur (Ludwig Van Beethoven), Annie Ducaux (Therese Von
    Brunswick), Jany Holt (Juliette Guicciardi), Yolande Lafon (Countess
    Guicciardi), Lucien Rozenberg (Count Guicciardi), Jean Debucourt
    (Count Gallenberg), Pauley (Schuppanzigh), Jean-Louis Barrault,
    Lucas Gridoux, Dalio, Roger Blin, André Nox, Gaston Dubosc, Jane
    Marken, Philippe Richard, Nadine Picard, Mary Lou, Rika Radifé.
    Released in the United States under the title *The Life and Loves of
    Beethoven*, November 1937.
16 mm. rental: To be distributed by Images Motion Picture Rental Library.
Cost: 2,000,000 francs. Shot in six weeks.

JÉRÓME PERREAU, HÉROS DES BARRICADES (Georges Milton, 1936)
Producer: Georges Milton.
Screenplay: Adapted from the novel by Henri Dupuy-Mazuel by Paúl Fékété.
Cinematographers: Roger Hubert and Lucas.
Assistants: Charpentier and Lalier.
Set decoration: Garnier and Bonamy.
Technical director: Baudouin.
Sound engineer: Royné.
Music: Score by Maurice Yvain.
Lyrics: Lucien Boyer.
Cast: Georges Milton (Jérôme Perreau), Robert Le Vigan (Cardinal Mazarin), Sanson Fainsilber (Archbishop of Gondi), Fernand Fabre (Duke of Beaufort), Jean Bara (Louis XIV), Serge Grave (Louis Perreau), Tania Fédor (Anne of Austria, Queen of France), Valentine Tessier (Duchess of Chevreuse), Iréne Brillant (Marie Perreau), Abel Tarride, Georges Mauloy, Bernard Lancret, Saint-Allier, Sellier, Mylo, janine Borelli, Jane Lamy, Saint-Hilaire, Mad Siamé.
Cost: 2,400,000 francs.
Shot in one month. Released in the United States under the title *The Queen and the Cardinal,* June 1944.

LE VOLEUR DE FEMMES (Films Union, 1936)
Screenplay: Abel Gance, based upon a novel by Pierre Frondaire.
Cinematographer: Roger Hubert.
Cast: Jules Berry, Jean Max, Jaque-Catelain, Gilbert Gil, Annie Ducaux, Lise Matrey, Sylvie Gance, Blanchette Brunoy, Mary Lou, Thomy Bourdelle (?).

J'ACCUSE (Société du film J'Accuse/Star Films, 1937)
Screenplay: Abel Gance and Steve Passeur.
Cinematographer: Roger Hubert.
Set decoration: Henri Mahé.
Music: Henri Verdun.
Cast: Victor Francen (Jean Diaz), Jean Max (Henri Chimay), Marcel Delaître (François Lorin), Paul Amiot (Captain), André Nox (Liotard), Georges Saillard (Gilles Tenant), Rollin (Pierre Fonds), Renée Devillers (Hélène), Mary Lou (Flo), Line Noro, Sylvie Gance, M. Cahuzac (?).
Cost: 4,300,000 francs.
This new sound version of the film was shot between May 14 and August 31, 1937. Released in the United States under the title *That They May Live,* November 1939.
Running time: 116 minutes.
16 mm. rental: Images Motion Picture Rental Library.

LOUISE (Société Parisienne de Production de Films, 1938)
Producers: Weyler and Goldinberg.
Screenplay: Abel Gance and Steve Passeur, based upon the opera by Gustave Charpentier.
Cinematographer: Kurt Currant.
Set decoration: Henri Mahé and George Wakhevitch.
Music: Gustave Charpentier.
Musical direction: Louis Beydts. Orchestra conducted by Eugene Bigot.
Editor: Léonide Azar.
Cast: Grace Moore (Louise), Suzanne Desprées (Mother), Ginette Leclerc (Lucienne), Pauline Carton (Forelady), Jacqueline Prévôt (Seamstress), Georges Thill (Julien), André Pernet (Father), Robert Le Vigan (Gaston), Jacqueline Gautier (Alphonsine), Rivers Cadet (Singer), Marcel Pérès (Sculptor), Edmond Beauchamp (Philosopher), Roger Blin.
Cost: 7,000,000 francs.
Shot during the months of November and December.

LE PARADIS PERDU (Taris Film, 1939)
Producer: Joseph Than.
Screenplay: Joseph Than and Abel Gance.
Dialogue: Steve Passeur.
Cinematographer: Christian Matras.
Set decoration: Henri Mahé.
Music: Hans May.
Editor: Léonide Azar.
Cast: Fernand Gravey (Pierre), Robert Le Vigan (Bordenave), Alerme (Calou), Micheline Presle (Janine/Jeanette), Elvire Popesco (Sonia, Princess Vorochine), Monique Rolland (Laura), Robert Pizani, Gérard Landry, Jean Brochard, Edmond Beauchamp, Palau, Jane Marken, Gaby Andreu, Roland Pégurier.
Released in the United States under the title *Four Flights to Love*, April 1942.

LA VÉNUS AVEUGLE (France-Nouvelle, 1940/41)
Producer: Fernand Rivers.
Cinematographers: L.-H. Burel and Alekan.
Assistant: Ed. T. Grevelle.
Set decoration: Henri Mahé and Paul Bertrand.
Music: Raoul Moretti.
Cast: Viviane Romance, Lucienne Lemarchand, Sylvie Gance, Marion Malville, Georges Flament, Henri Guisol, Aquistapace, Roland Pégurier.
Cost: 4,100,000 francs.

LE CAPITAINE FRACASSE (Lux-films, 1942)
Screenplay: Abel Gance and Claude Vermorel, from the novel by Théophile
    Gautier.
Cinematographer: Nicolas Hayer.
Set decoration: Henri Mahé.
Music: Arthur Honegger.
Cast: Fernand Gravey, Jean Weber, Paul Oettly, Maurice Escande, Roland
    Toutain, Roger Blin, Lucien Nat, Assia Noris, Vina Bovy, Mona Goya,
    Alice Tissot, Sylvie Gance, Andrée Guize.

QUATORZE JUILLET 1953 (Rosetti/Gaumont/Debrie, 1953/54)
Producers: Georges Rosetti, with Gaumont and André Debrie.
Assistant: Jean Debrix.
Editor: Jacques Chastel. First experiment of Polyvision in color; later in-
    cluded as part of the *Magirama* spectacle (see below).
Running time: Twenty minutes.
Premiere: Gaumont-Palace, July 15, 1954.

LA TOUR DE NESLE (Fernand Rivers, 1954)
Producer: Fernand Rivers.
Screenplay: Abel Gance, adapted from the original story by Alexandre
    Dumas père and Gaillardet.
Dialogue: Abel Gance, Fernand Rivers, Etienne Fuzellier.
Assistants: Michel Boisrond, Yvan Jouannet.
Cinematographer: André Thomas.
Set decoration: René Bouladoux.
Costumes: Mme. Martinez.
Music: Henri Verdun.
Editor: Mme. Taverna.
Cast: Pierre Brasseur, Paul Guers, Jacques Toja, Michel Bouquet, Marcel
    Raine, Michel Etchevery, Maffioly, the younger Rivers, Paul De-
    mange, Gabriello, Rellys, Jacques Meyran, Nelly Kaplan, Sylvana
    Pampanini, Lia di Leo, Christina Grado, Claude Sylvain.
Shot in Gévacolor during August and September.

MAGIRAMA (Abel Gance and Nelly Kaplan, 1956)
Producers: Abel Gance, in collaboration with Nelly Kaplan.
Made up of the following episodes: *Auprès de ma Blonde, Château de
    Nuages, Fête foraine, J'Accuse, 14 juillet.* A demonstration of the spec-
    tacular potential of "Polyvision" and the "Triple Screen," incorporating
    scenes from earlier films (such as *J'Accuse*). Testing the future of
    Polyvision, Gance anticipated the day when mass cinematic spectacles
    would overwhelm as many as 20,000 spectators at a time. As he wrote
    for *Cahiers du Cinéma* (December 1954), "Le cinéma, qu'on le veuille

ou non, est en marche vers ces grands spectacles où l'esprit des peuples se forgera sur l'enclume d'un art collectif."

AUSTERLITZ (1960)
Co-director: Roger Richebé.
Screenplay: Abel Gance, in collaboration with Nelly Kaplan.
Cinematographers: Henri Alekan and Robert Juillard.
Music: Jean Ledru.
Cast: Pierre Mondy (Napoléon), Martine Carol (Joséphine), Claudia Cardinale (Pauline), Elvire Popesco (Mme. Letizia), Jean Mercure (Talleyrand), Orson Welles (Fulton), Leslie Caron (Mme. de Vaudrey), Vittorio De Sica (Pie VII), Polycarpe Pavloff (Koutousof), Rossano Brazzi (Lucien Bonaparte), Jean Marais (Carnot), George Marchal (Lannes), J.-L. Horbette (Constant), Nelly Kaplan (Mme. Récamier), Michel Simon, Jack Palance, Ettore Nenni, J.-L. Trintignant, J.-M. Bory, Jacques Castelot, André Certes, Randall, Lucien Raimbourg, Anthony Stuart, Louis Eymond, Maurice Teynac, Anne-Marie Ferrero, Daniela Rocca.

CYRANO ET D'ARTAGNAN (Cine-Agata Film Productions/Circe-Astarte, 1963)
Screenplay: Abel Gance and Nelly Kaplan.
Cinematographers: Otello Martelli and Picon-Borel.
Cast: José Ferrer (Cyrano de Bergerac), Jean-Pierre Cassel (D'Artagnan), Dahlia Lavi (Marion), Sylva Koscina (Ninon), Michel Simon (Duc de Mauvières), Ivo Garrani (Laubardemont), Philippe Noiret (Louis XIII), Laura Valenzuela (The Queen), Rafael Rivelles (Richelieu), Mario Passante, Polidor, Guy Henry, Bob Morel, Vanni Lisenti, Barco Bari, David Montemuri, André Lauriault, Vincent Parca, Carlo Dori, et al.
Running time: 145 minutes.

BONAPARTE ET LA REVOLUTION (Les Films 13/Claude Lelouch, 1971)
Producers: Abel Gance in collaboration with Claude Lelouch.
Prologue: Abel Gance (at the age of 82).
Narrator: Jean Topart.
Post-synch: Claude Pessis.
Cast: Albert Dieudonné, Edmond van Daele, Alexandre Koubitsky, Antonin Artaud, Abel Gance, and other players of the 1926 version (excluding the childhood sequences) and of the sound version of 1934.
This remake utilizes footage from the earlier versions of *Napoléon* and provides some additional new material.
Running time: 235 minutes.
16 mm. rental: Images Motion Picture Rental Library.

5. Major Unrealized Projects

ECCE HOMO: Begun and interrupted, 1915. Gance later refers to *Ecce Homo* (along with *Le Royaume de la Terre* and *La Fin du Monde*) in *Prisme* as "my great and only cinematographic hopes for the next two years." He still considered *Ecce Home* his "great mission" in 1972.
LE SOLEIL NOIR: Le Film d'Art production interrupted March, 1918. Cinematography: L.-H. Burel. Cast: Berthe Bady, Mme. Dourgas, Silvio de Pedrelli.
LA SOCIÉTÉ DES NATIONS; LES CICATRICES; LE ROYAUME DE LA TERRE (1917–27). All of them are important; the latter was meant to create a new synthesis of Faith through the cinema.
LES GRANDS INITIÉS: BOUDDHA, KRISHNA, CONFUCIUS, MOÏSE, SIVA DE DANSEUR, JĒSUS, MAHOMET, LUTHER, LAMARCK: This scenario, conceived in 1928, was intended to proclaim the ecumenicism of the religions of the world.
LA DIVINE TRAGÉDIE (1937–47): Derived from the Christ episode of *Les Grands Initiés*, this project was to be executed in Polyvision. According to Philippe Esnault, all that remained (in the mid-1950s) were the models of the art director Mazereel.
CHRISTOPHE COLOMB (1939): Scenario and dialogue written in collaboration with Steve Passeur. Sets by Henri Mahé. Costumes by Robert Baldrich. Music by Joaquin Rodrigo and Henri Verdun. Shooting for this film was to have started June 12, 1939, on location in Granada. In later years Gance has done much further work on this script.
MANOLETE (1944): Cinematography: Guerner. This unfinished film was begun in Spain in 1944.
BLEU-BLANC-ROUGE (1940).
LA FIAMETTA (1941).
ISABELLE LA CATHOLIQUE (1941).

6. Major Inventions by Abel Gance

Écran panoramique triple de l'écran ordinaire, polyvision et écran variable. Patent No. 633.415, dated August 20, 1926; improved by Patent No. 35.034.

Perspective sonore. Patent No. 280.255, dated August 13, 1929; improved by Patent No. 35.034, dated March 10, 1932, registered with André Debrie.

Pictographe. Patent No. 833.904, dated August 1, 1938.

Index